Su Doku Solver

The unique grid system and know-how to help you crack the hit Japanese number puzzle game

OLIVER PITT

Capella

This edition published in 2005 by Arcturus Publishing Limited
26/27 Bickels Yard, 151–153 Bermondsey Street,
London SE1 3HA

In Canada published for Indigo Books
468 King St W,
Suite 500,
Toronto,
Ontario M5V 1L8

ISBN 1-84193-374-0

Printed in England

INTRODUCTION

The Japanese craze Su Doku – sometimes called Sudoku – is now a global phenomenon. The idea on which Su Doku is based first emerged in a US puzzle magazine. It was then adapted by Nikoli in Japan who gave it the name Su Doku – Su meaning number, and Doku meaning single. In any language the game is challenging. Many puzzlers give it up through sheer frustration, while others become addicted to the thrill of correctly filling the blank cells in the unique Su Doku grid. This book aims to help the beginner get off to a flying start as well as assist the Su Doku addict to hone his or her skills.

There can only be one solution to a Su Doku puzzle, which is why the genre presents such a challenge. Place one number in the wrong cell and the whole puzzle is wrong. The *Su Doku Solver* should prevent you wasting time, by enabling you to plot out each puzzle. We'll show you how this component of the Solver works later, but first let's look at the basics of doing Su Doku, beginning with what the game actually requires of you, and the tools you have to work with.

UNDERSTANDING THE GRID

It is absolutely vital that you are familiar with the basic grid and its composition. Unless you know it inside out you won't be able to work effectively with it.

The unique Su Doku grid comprises nine linked blocks each of which incorporates nine cells. The blocks are numbered 1 through to 9, starting at top left. Similarly each row and column is numbered 1 through to 9.

The aim of the game is to fill in the grid so that every row, every column, and every box contains the digits 1 to 9. This might seem simple enough, but it can be very frustrating, especially with puzzles at the highest level of difficulty.

Study the composition of the basic grid below, then move on.

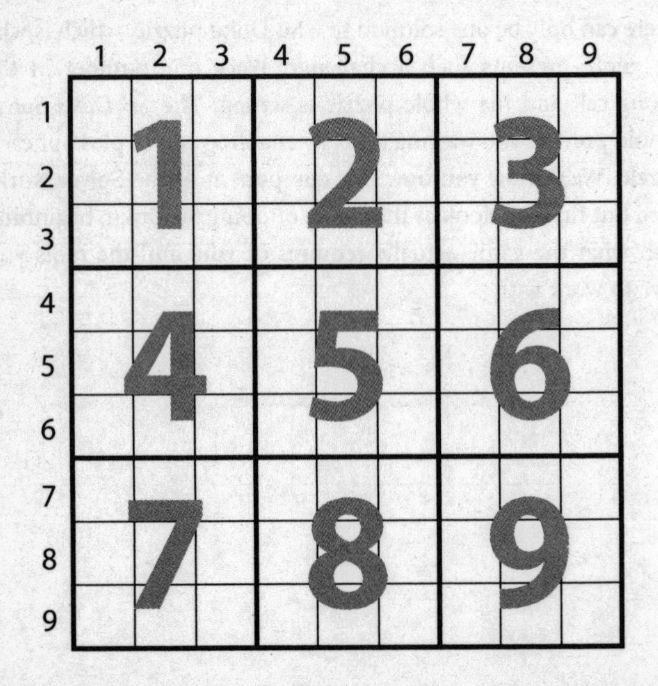

SCANNING THE GRID

Each fresh Su Doku puzzle comes with a number, or numbers, in each column or row within each block of the grid, to get you started. The challenge is to fill in the blank cells with the missing numbers. To complete the puzzle there must be one number – from 1 to 9 – in each column, row and block. Begin by scanning the grid in all directions (see example below): along the rows, up and down the columns and in each of the nine blocks. The same number cannot appear more than once in the same row, column or block. The idea of the puzzle is number placement in a symmetrical sequence.

	6	5	9			3		
				6	7	9		
	4		3					1
		6		5			9	4
		9	4		2			
					4		1	
		8	5	7				6
		1		9		8	3	

NARROWING YOUR OPTIONS

Now let's take a real puzzle. First, check the top three blocks, identify the blanks, and scan down each of the columns and across each of the rows. Note that the middle and bottom blocks in the centre (blocks 5 and 8) already contain the number 5, in columns 4 and 5. There must, therefore, be a number 5 in the top centre block, and its correct position must be column 6 (labelled A in the example below).

← COLUMNS →

↑ ROWS ↓

	C1	C2	C3	C4	C5	C6	C7	C8	C9
R1		6		9		8	3		
R2	2				6	7	9		
R3		4		3		A			1
R4			6		5			9	4
R5				4		2			
R6	7				8		1		
R7	6					4		1	
R8			8	5	7				6
R9			1		9		8	3	

C = Column
R = Row

In central block 5 (shaded in the example below), in the top and bottom cells in column 6, there are two spaces, labelled B and C. Look at columns 4 and 5 and you will find a number 9. It follows that number 9 in block 5 must be placed in either B or C. You can discover which by looking across rows 4, 5 and 6, where you will see a number 9 in row 4. The number 9 you are looking for in block 5 therefore fits, appropriately, into cell 9, labelled C.

An understanding of the methods for working out the correct solution for Su Doku is essential, but in the heat of battle with a real live puzzle you will need more than mere methodology.

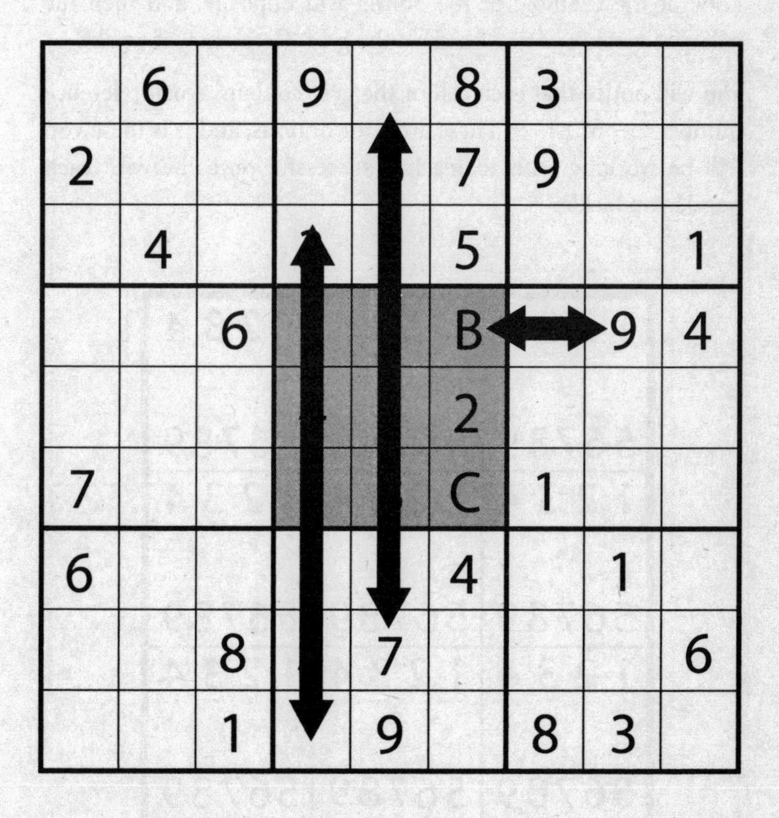

THE SOLVER GRID

Examples 3 and 4 should have proved to you that having a strategy to help you eliminate possibilities is key to success in solving Su Doku puzzles.

But you also need something else, something very practical – a way of remembering the numerous options that will crowd your brain each time you concentrate on a Su Doku puzzle. Enter the Su Doku Solver. Based on the standard Su Doku grid, it has been designed to enable you to recall those myriad options instantly.

Look at the example of the Solver grid opposite, and then the enlarged version of one block of the grid. Here's how it works.

You will notice that each cell of the grid contains small reference numbers, from 1 to 9. These are your options, and it is these you will be working with to reach a successful outcome with each puzzle you tackle.

1 2 3 4 56789	1 2 3 4 56789	1 2 3 4 56789
1 2 3 4 56789	1 2 3 4 56789	1 2 3 4 56789
1 2 3 4 56789	1 2 3 4 56789	1 2 3 4 56789

1 2 3 4 56789	1 2 3 4 56789	1 2 3 4 56789	1 2 3 4 56789	1 2 3 4 56789	1 2 3 4 56789	1 2 3 4 56789	1 2 3 4 56789	1 2 3 4 56789
1 2 3 4 56789	1 2 3 4 56789	1 2 3 4 56789	1 2 3 4 56789	1 2 3 4 56789	1 2 3 4 56789	1 2 3 4 56789	1 2 3 4 56789	1 2 3 4 56789
1 2 3 4 56789	1 2 3 4 56789	1 2 3 4 56789	1 2 3 4 56789	1 2 3 4 56789	1 2 3 4 56789	1 2 3 4 56789	1 2 3 4 56789	1 2 3 4 56789
1 2 3 4 56789	1 2 3 4 56789	1 2 3 4 56789	1 2 3 4 56789	1 2 3 4 56789	1 2 3 4 56789	1 2 3 4 56789	1 2 3 4 56789	1 2 3 4 56789
1 2 3 4 56789	1 2 3 4 56789	1 2 3 4 56789	1 2 3 4 56789	1 2 3 4 56789	1 2 3 4 56789	1 2 3 4 56789	1 2 3 4 56789	1 2 3 4 56789
1 2 3 4 56789	1 2 3 4 56789	1 2 3 4 56789	1 2 3 4 56789	1 2 3 4 56789	1 2 3 4 56789	1 2 3 4 56789	1 2 3 4 56789	1 2 3 4 56789
1 2 3 4 56789	1 2 3 4 56789	1 2 3 4 56789	1 2 3 4 56789	1 2 3 4 56789	1 2 3 4 56789	1 2 3 4 56789	1 2 3 4 56789	1 2 3 4 56789
1 2 3 4 56789	1 2 3 4 56789	1 2 3 4 56789	1 2 3 4 56789	1 2 3 4 56789	1 2 3 4 56789	1 2 3 4 56789	1 2 3 4 56789	1 2 3 4 56789
1 2 3 4 56789	1 2 3 4 56789	1 2 3 4 56789	1 2 3 4 56789	1 2 3 4 56789	1 2 3 4 56789	1 2 3 4 56789	1 2 3 4 56789	1 2 3 4 56789

HOW TO USE THE SOLVER

Let's assume you want to start a puzzle. Begin by transferring the numbers supplied in the puzzle to a blank grid in the Grids section (see example opposite).

Delete the transferred numbers from the 1-9 sequence in each of the blank cells. The same number can not appear more than once in the same column, row or block, so you must ensure that, once a particular number appears in a column or row, that you strike out its reference number counterpart in the blank cells of the Solver grid.

Now begin to work out the puzzle, scanning the rows and columns across all blocks. As you work, you will gradually narrow your options through a process of elimination, and this is where the small reference numbers really help.

The more complex the Su Doku the more options you will find yourself having to assess. In these situations some form of annotation to help you keep track of the options is vital. You may even find that you need to plot out the various options confronting you, using the blank grids to see which number placements work. When you are presented with several options, this is the only sure way of solving a puzzle.

1234 3 56789	1234 1 56789	1234 56789	1234 4 56789	1234 56789	1234 8 56789	1234 56789	1234 56789	1234 56789
1234 56789	1234 56789	1234 2 56789	1234 56789	1234 56789	1234 56789	1234 56789	1234 3 56789	1234 9 56789
1234 56789	1234 9 56789	1234 56789	1234 3 56789	1234 56789	1234 56789	1234 1 56789	1234 56789	1234 56789
1234 7 56789	1234 56789	1234 1 56789	1234 9 56789	1234 56789	1234 4 56789	1234 56789	1234 5 56789	1234 6 56789
1234 56789	1234 5 56789	1234 56789	1234 56789	1234 3 56789	1234 56789	1234 56789	1234 56789	1234 56789
1234 9 56789	1234 6 56789	1234 56789	1234 7 56789	1234 8 56789	1234 56789	1234 56789	1234 56789	1234 56789
1234 4 56789	1234 56789	1234 5 56789	1234 8 56789	1234 1 56789	1234 56789	1234 56789	1234 6 56789	1234 56789
1234 56789	1234 56789	1234 56789	1234 56789	1234 56789	1234 3 56789	1234 56789	1234 56789	1234 56789
1234 6 56789	1234 56789	1234 3 56789	1234 56789	1234 56789	1234 7 56789	1234 56789	1234 56789	1234 56789

PRACTISE MAKES PERFECT

Su Dokus come in varying degrees of difficulty. The six sample puzzles shown on the following few pages represent the three normal gradings. Try all six and you will soon get a feel for the characteristics of each grade. This isn't meant as a test of your prowess in Su Doku, but to demonstrate how a seemingly simple puzzle can be developed into a formidable challenge. The puzzle rating is subjective. No two minds are the same. You might struggle for hours on an easy puzzle but skip through a hard puzzle. I have rated the examples according to how I solve puzzles and the strategies I have developed. Using the Solver, and with practise, you will find it easier and quicker to complete even the most testing puzzle. Good luck!

Easy Puzzle 1

3	1		4		8			
		2					3	9
	9		3			1		
7		1	9		4		5	6
	5			3				
9	6		7	8				
4		5	8	1			6	
					3			
6		3			7			

Easy Puzzle 2

					3	7	8	6
9		3	6					
4		8		2	7			9
	3	5	8			4	9	1
					4			7
7		2		9	1	8		3
				3	8	1		5
		4					7	8
		7	4	1			3	2

Medium Puzzle 1

4	5				7		3	2
			4		1			
1		9			5	4		8
	6			9	3	2	4	1
9	4			1	6	5		3
		4			2		1	6
2		1			8	9		
		6	1				2	

Medium Puzzle 2

		9			6	7	2	3
1					7			4
	6	7						9
	9	5	2				1	7
						2		
	4				1			5
	8	1				5	6	2
5								1
2		6	1		9			8

Hard Puzzle 1

		3						
		9					7	6
	4		5					
		6	2			5		1
3		5					2	
1							8	
4		8						2
	5	2						
				5			6	3

Hard Puzzle 2

		4			1			
	6							
					8	5		9
7		8					5	1
					7			
				1	9		8	6
	8	1				9		4
			1		4			5

Easy Puzzle 1 Solution

3	1	6	4	9	8	7	2	5
8	4	2	5	7	1	6	3	9
5	9	7	3	6	2	1	4	8
7	3	1	9	2	4	8	5	6
2	5	8	1	3	6	9	7	4
9	6	4	7	8	5	2	1	3
4	7	5	8	1	9	3	6	2
1	2	9	6	4	3	5	8	7
6	8	3	2	5	7	4	9	1

Easy Puzzle 2 Solution

5	2	1	9	4	3	7	8	6
9	7	3	6	8	5	2	1	4
4	6	8	1	2	7	3	5	9
6	3	5	8	7	2	4	9	1
1	8	9	3	6	4	5	2	7
7	4	2	5	9	1	8	6	3
2	9	6	7	3	8	1	4	5
3	1	4	2	5	6	9	7	8
8	5	7	4	1	9	6	3	2

Medium Puzzle 1 Solution

4	5	8	9	6	7	1	3	2
6	2	3	4	8	1	7	9	5
1	7	9	2	3	5	4	6	8
8	6	5	7	9	3	2	4	1
3	1	7	5	2	4	6	8	9
9	4	2	8	1	6	5	7	3
7	9	4	3	5	2	8	1	6
2	3	1	6	4	8	9	5	7
5	8	6	1	7	9	3	2	4

Medium Puzzle 2 Solution

4	5	9	8	1	6	7	2	3
1	2	8	9	3	7	6	5	4
3	6	7	4	2	5	1	8	9
6	9	5	2	4	3	8	1	7
7	1	3	5	9	8	2	4	6
8	4	2	7	6	1	9	3	5
9	8	1	3	7	4	5	6	2
5	7	4	6	8	2	3	9	1
2	3	6	1	5	9	4	7	8

Hard Puzzle 1 Solution

8	6	3	9	7	1	2	4	5
5	1	9	4	2	3	8	7	6
2	4	7	5	6	8	1	3	9
7	8	6	2	3	4	5	9	1
3	9	5	1	8	7	6	2	4
1	2	4	6	9	5	3	8	7
4	3	8	7	1	6	9	5	2
6	5	2	3	4	9	7	1	8
9	7	1	8	5	2	4	6	3

Hard Puzzle 2 Solution

9	5	4	7	3	1	2	6	8
8	6	7	9	5	2	1	4	3
1	2	3	4	6	8	5	7	9
7	9	8	3	2	6	4	5	1
5	1	6	8	4	7	3	9	2
4	3	2	5	1	9	7	8	6
2	8	1	6	7	5	9	3	4
6	4	5	2	9	3	8	1	7
3	7	9	1	8	4	6	2	5

1 2 3 4 56789	1 2 3 4 56789	1 2 3 4 56789	1 2 3 4 56789	1 2 3 4 56789	1 2 3 4 56789	1 2 3 4 56789	1 2 3 4 56789	1 2 3 4 56789
1 2 3 4 56789	1 2 3 4 56789	1 2 3 4 56789	1 2 3 4 56789	1 2 3 4 56789	1 2 3 4 56789	1 2 3 4 56789	1 2 3 4 56789	1 2 3 4 56789
1 2 3 4 56789	1 2 3 4 56789	1 2 3 4 56789	1 2 3 4 56789	1 2 3 4 56789	1 2 3 4 56789	1 2 3 4 56789	1 2 3 4 56789	1 2 3 4 56789
1 2 3 4 56789	1 2 3 4 56789	1 2 3 4 56789	1 2 3 4 56789	1 2 3 4 56789	1 2 3 4 56789	1 2 3 4 56789	1 2 3 4 56789	1 2 3 4 56789
1 2 3 4 56789	1 2 3 4 56789	1 2 3 4 56789	1 2 3 4 56789	1 2 3 4 56789	1 2 3 4 56789	1 2 3 4 56789	1 2 3 4 56789	1 2 3 4 56789
1 2 3 4 56789	1 2 3 4 56789	1 2 3 4 56789	1 2 3 4 56789	1 2 3 4 56789	1 2 3 4 56789	1 2 3 4 56789	1 2 3 4 56789	1 2 3 4 56789
1 2 3 4 56789	1 2 3 4 56789	1 2 3 4 56789	1 2 3 4 56789	1 2 3 4 56789	1 2 3 4 56789	1 2 3 4 56789	1 2 3 4 56789	1 2 3 4 56789
1 2 3 4 56789	1 2 3 4 56789	1 2 3 4 56789	1 2 3 4 56789	1 2 3 4 56789	1 2 3 4 56789	1 2 3 4 56789	1 2 3 4 56789	1 2 3 4 56789
1 2 3 4 56789	1 2 3 4 56789	1 2 3 4 56789	1 2 3 4 56789	1 2 3 4 56789	1 2 3 4 56789	1 2 3 4 56789	1 2 3 4 56789	1 2 3 4 56789

1 2 3 4 56789	1 2 3 4 56789	1 2 3 4 56789	1 2 3 4 56789	1 2 3 4 56789	1 2 3 4 56789	1 2 3 4 56789	1 2 3 4 56789	1 2 3 4 56789
1 2 3 4 56789	1 2 3 4 56789	1 2 3 4 56789	1 2 3 4 56789	1 2 3 4 56789	1 2 3 4 56789	1 2 3 4 56789	1 2 3 4 56789	1 2 3 4 56789
1 2 3 4 56789	1 2 3 4 56789	1 2 3 4 56789	1 2 3 4 56789	1 2 3 4 56789	1 2 3 4 56789	1 2 3 4 56789	1 2 3 4 56789	1 2 3 4 56789
1 2 3 4 56789	1 2 3 4 56789	1 2 3 4 56789	1 2 3 4 56789	1 2 3 4 56789	1 2 3 4 56789	1 2 3 4 56789	1 2 3 4 56789	1 2 3 4 56789
1 2 3 4 56789	1 2 3 4 56789	1 2 3 4 56789	1 2 3 4 56789	1 2 3 4 56789	1 2 3 4 56789	1 2 3 4 56789	1 2 3 4 56789	1 2 3 4 56789
1 2 3 4 56789	1 2 3 4 56789	1 2 3 4 56789	1 2 3 4 56789	1 2 3 4 56789	1 2 3 4 56789	1 2 3 4 56789	1 2 3 4 56789	1 2 3 4 56789
1 2 3 4 56789	1 2 3 4 56789	1 2 3 4 56789	1 2 3 4 56789	1 2 3 4 56789	1 2 3 4 56789	1 2 3 4 56789	1 2 3 4 56789	1 2 3 4 56789
1 2 3 4 56789	1 2 3 4 56789	1 2 3 4 56789	1 2 3 4 56789	1 2 3 4 56789	1 2 3 4 56789	1 2 3 4 56789	1 2 3 4 56789	1 2 3 4 56789
1 2 3 4 56789	1 2 3 4 56789	1 2 3 4 56789	1 2 3 4 56789	1 2 3 4 56789	1 2 3 4 56789	1 2 3 4 56789	1 2 3 4 56789	1 2 3 4 56789

1 2 3 4 56789	1 2 3 4 56789	1 2 3 4 56789	1 2 3 4 56789	1 2 3 4 56789	1 2 3 4 56789	1 2 3 4 56789	1 2 3 4 56789	1 2 3 4 56789
1 2 3 4 56789	1 2 3 4 56789	1 2 3 4 56789	1 2 3 4 56789	1 2 3 4 56789	1 2 3 4 56789	1 2 3 4 56789	1 2 3 4 56789	1 2 3 4 56789
1 2 3 4 56789	1 2 3 4 56789	1 2 3 4 56789	1 2 3 4 56789	1 2 3 4 56789	1 2 3 4 56789	1 2 3 4 56789	1 2 3 4 56789	1 2 3 4 56789
1 2 3 4 56789	1 2 3 4 56789	1 2 3 4 56789	1 2 3 4 56789	1 2 3 4 56789	1 2 3 4 56789	1 2 3 4 56789	1 2 3 4 56789	1 2 3 4 56789
1 2 3 4 56789	1 2 3 4 56789	1 2 3 4 56789	1 2 3 4 56789	1 2 3 4 56789	1 2 3 4 56789	1 2 3 4 56789	1 2 3 4 56789	1 2 3 4 56789
1 2 3 4 56789	1 2 3 4 56789	1 2 3 4 56789	1 2 3 4 56789	1 2 3 4 56789	1 2 3 4 56789	1 2 3 4 56789	1 2 3 4 56789	1 2 3 4 56789
1 2 3 4 56789	1 2 3 4 56789	1 2 3 4 56789	1 2 3 4 56789	1 2 3 4 56789	1 2 3 4 56789	1 2 3 4 56789	1 2 3 4 56789	1 2 3 4 56789
1 2 3 4 56789	1 2 3 4 56789	1 2 3 4 56789	1 2 3 4 56789	1 2 3 4 56789	1 2 3 4 56789	1 2 3 4 56789	1 2 3 4 56789	1 2 3 4 56789
1 2 3 4 56789	1 2 3 4 56789	1 2 3 4 56789	1 2 3 4 56789	1 2 3 4 56789	1 2 3 4 56789	1 2 3 4 56789	1 2 3 4 56789	1 2 3 4 56789

1 2 3 4 56789	1 2 3 4 56789	1 2 3 4 56789	1 2 3 4 56789	1 2 3 4 56789	1 2 3 4 56789	1 2 3 4 56789	1 2 3 4 56789	1 2 3 4 56789
1 2 3 4 56789	1 2 3 4 56789	1 2 3 4 56789	1 2 3 4 56789	1 2 3 4 56789	1 2 3 4 56789	1 2 3 4 56789	1 2 3 4 56789	1 2 3 4 56789
1 2 3 4 56789	1 2 3 4 56789	1 2 3 4 56789	1 2 3 4 56789	1 2 3 4 56789	1 2 3 4 56789	1 2 3 4 56789	1 2 3 4 56789	1 2 3 4 56789
1 2 3 4 56789	1 2 3 4 56789	1 2 3 4 56789	1 2 3 4 56789	1 2 3 4 56789	1 2 3 4 56789	1 2 3 4 56789	1 2 3 4 56789	1 2 3 4 56789
1 2 3 4 56789	1 2 3 4 56789	1 2 3 4 56789	1 2 3 4 56789	1 2 3 4 56789	1 2 3 4 56789	1 2 3 4 56789	1 2 3 4 56789	1 2 3 4 56789
1 2 3 4 56789	1 2 3 4 56789	1 2 3 4 56789	1 2 3 4 56789	1 2 3 4 56789	1 2 3 4 56789	1 2 3 4 56789	1 2 3 4 56789	1 2 3 4 56789
1 2 3 4 56789	1 2 3 4 56789	1 2 3 4 56789	1 2 3 4 56789	1 2 3 4 56789	1 2 3 4 56789	1 2 3 4 56789	1 2 3 4 56789	1 2 3 4 56789
1 2 3 4 56789	1 2 3 4 56789	1 2 3 4 56789	1 2 3 4 56789	1 2 3 4 56789	1 2 3 4 56789	1 2 3 4 56789	1 2 3 4 56789	1 2 3 4 56789
1 2 3 4 56789	1 2 3 4 56789	1 2 3 4 56789	1 2 3 4 56789	1 2 3 4 56789	1 2 3 4 56789	1 2 3 4 56789	1 2 3 4 56789	1 2 3 4 56789

1 2 3 4 56789	1 2 3 4 56789	1 2 3 4 56789	1 2 3 4 56789	1 2 3 4 56789	1 2 3 4 56789	1 2 3 4 56789	1 2 3 4 56789	1 2 3 4 56789
1 2 3 4 56789	1 2 3 4 56789	1 2 3 4 56789	1 2 3 4 56789	1 2 3 4 56789	1 2 3 4 56789	1 2 3 4 56789	1 2 3 4 56789	1 2 3 4 56789
1 2 3 4 56789	1 2 3 4 56789	1 2 3 4 56789	1 2 3 4 56789	1 2 3 4 56789	1 2 3 4 56789	1 2 3 4 56789	1 2 3 4 56789	1 2 3 4 56789
1 2 3 4 56789	1 2 3 4 56789	1 2 3 4 56789	1 2 3 4 56789	1 2 3 4 56789	1 2 3 4 56789	1 2 3 4 56789	1 2 3 4 56789	1 2 3 4 56789
1 2 3 4 56789	1 2 3 4 56789	1 2 3 4 56789	1 2 3 4 56789	1 2 3 4 56789	1 2 3 4 56789	1 2 3 4 56789	1 2 3 4 56789	1 2 3 4 56789
1 2 3 4 56789	1 2 3 4 56789	1 2 3 4 56789	1 2 3 4 56789	1 2 3 4 56789	1 2 3 4 56789	1 2 3 4 56789	1 2 3 4 56789	1 2 3 4 56789
1 2 3 4 56789	1 2 3 4 56789	1 2 3 4 56789	1 2 3 4 56789	1 2 3 4 56789	1 2 3 4 56789	1 2 3 4 56789	1 2 3 4 56789	1 2 3 4 56789
1 2 3 4 56789	1 2 3 4 56789	1 2 3 4 56789	1 2 3 4 56789	1 2 3 4 56789	1 2 3 4 56789	1 2 3 4 56789	1 2 3 4 56789	1 2 3 4 56789
1 2 3 4 56789	1 2 3 4 56789	1 2 3 4 56789	1 2 3 4 56789	1 2 3 4 56789	1 2 3 4 56789	1 2 3 4 56789	1 2 3 4 56789	1 2 3 4 56789

1 2 3 4 56789	1 2 3 4 56789	1 2 3 4 56789	1 2 3 4 56789	1 2 3 4 56789	1 2 3 4 56789	1 2 3 4 56789	1 2 3 4 56789	1 2 3 4 56789
1 2 3 4 56789	1 2 3 4 56789	1 2 3 4 56789	1 2 3 4 56789	1 2 3 4 56789	1 2 3 4 56789	1 2 3 4 56789	1 2 3 4 56789	1 2 3 4 56789
1 2 3 4 56789	1 2 3 4 56789	1 2 3 4 56789	1 2 3 4 56789	1 2 3 4 56789	1 2 3 4 56789	1 2 3 4 56789	1 2 3 4 56789	1 2 3 4 56789
1 2 3 4 56789	1 2 3 4 56789	1 2 3 4 56789	1 2 3 4 56789	1 2 3 4 56789	1 2 3 4 56789	1 2 3 4 56789	1 2 3 4 56789	1 2 3 4 56789
1 2 3 4 56789	1 2 3 4 56789	1 2 3 4 56789	1 2 3 4 56789	1 2 3 4 56789	1 2 3 4 56789	1 2 3 4 56789	1 2 3 4 56789	1 2 3 4 56789
1 2 3 4 56789	1 2 3 4 56789	1 2 3 4 56789	1 2 3 4 56789	1 2 3 4 56789	1 2 3 4 56789	1 2 3 4 56789	1 2 3 4 56789	1 2 3 4 56789
1 2 3 4 56789	1 2 3 4 56789	1 2 3 4 56789	1 2 3 4 56789	1 2 3 4 56789	1 2 3 4 56789	1 2 3 4 56789	1 2 3 4 56789	1 2 3 4 56789
1 2 3 4 56789	1 2 3 4 56789	1 2 3 4 56789	1 2 3 4 56789	1 2 3 4 56789	1 2 3 4 56789	1 2 3 4 56789	1 2 3 4 56789	1 2 3 4 56789
1 2 3 4 56789	1 2 3 4 56789	1 2 3 4 56789	1 2 3 4 56789	1 2 3 4 56789	1 2 3 4 56789	1 2 3 4 56789	1 2 3 4 56789	1 2 3 4 56789

1234 56789	1234 56789	1234 56789	1234 56789	1234 56789	1234 56789	1234 56789	1234 56789	1234 56789
1234 56789	1234 56789	1234 56789	1234 56789	1234 56789	1234 56789	1234 56789	1234 56789	1234 56789
1234 56789	1234 56789	1234 56789	1234 56789	1234 56789	1234 56789	1234 56789	1234 56789	1234 56789
1234 56789	1234 56789	1234 56789	1234 56789	1234 56789	1234 56789	1234 56789	1234 56789	1234 56789
1234 56789	1234 56789	1234 56789	1234 56789	1234 56789	1234 56789	1234 56789	1234 56789	1234 56789
1234 56789	1234 56789	1234 56789	1234 56789	1234 56789	1234 56789	1234 56789	1234 56789	1234 56789
1234 56789	1234 56789	1234 56789	1234 56789	1234 56789	1234 56789	1234 56789	1234 56789	1234 56789
1234 56789	1234 56789	1234 56789	1234 56789	1234 56789	1234 56789	1234 56789	1234 56789	1234 56789
1234 56789	1234 56789	1234 56789	1234 56789	1234 56789	1234 56789	1234 56789	1234 56789	1234 56789

1 2 3 4 56789	1 2 3 4 56789	1 2 3 4 56789	1 2 3 4 56789	1 2 3 4 56789	1 2 3 4 56789	1 2 3 4 56789	1 2 3 4 56789	1 2 3 4 56789
1 2 3 4 56789	1 2 3 4 56789	1 2 3 4 56789	1 2 3 4 56789	1 2 3 4 56789	1 2 3 4 56789	1 2 3 4 56789	1 2 3 4 56789	1 2 3 4 56789
1 2 3 4 56789	1 2 3 4 56789	1 2 3 4 56789	1 2 3 4 56789	1 2 3 4 56789	1 2 3 4 56789	1 2 3 4 56789	1 2 3 4 56789	1 2 3 4 56789
1 2 3 4 56789	1 2 3 4 56789	1 2 3 4 56789	1 2 3 4 56789	1 2 3 4 56789	1 2 3 4 56789	1 2 3 4 56789	1 2 3 4 56789	1 2 3 4 56789
1 2 3 4 56789	1 2 3 4 56789	1 2 3 4 56789	1 2 3 4 56789	1 2 3 4 56789	1 2 3 4 56789	1 2 3 4 56789	1 2 3 4 56789	1 2 3 4 56789
1 2 3 4 56789	1 2 3 4 56789	1 2 3 4 56789	1 2 3 4 56789	1 2 3 4 56789	1 2 3 4 56789	1 2 3 4 56789	1 2 3 4 56789	1 2 3 4 56789
1 2 3 4 56789	1 2 3 4 56789	1 2 3 4 56789	1 2 3 4 56789	1 2 3 4 56789	1 2 3 4 56789	1 2 3 4 56789	1 2 3 4 56789	1 2 3 4 56789
1 2 3 4 56789	1 2 3 4 56789	1 2 3 4 56789	1 2 3 4 56789	1 2 3 4 56789	1 2 3 4 56789	1 2 3 4 56789	1 2 3 4 56789	1 2 3 4 56789
1 2 3 4 56789	1 2 3 4 56789	1 2 3 4 56789	1 2 3 4 56789	1 2 3 4 56789	1 2 3 4 56789	1 2 3 4 56789	1 2 3 4 56789	1 2 3 4 56789

1 2 3 4 56789	1 2 3 4 56789	1 2 3 4 56789	1 2 3 4 56789	1 2 3 4 56789	1 2 3 4 56789	1 2 3 4 56789	1 2 3 4 56789	1 2 3 4 56789
1 2 3 4 56789	1 2 3 4 56789	1 2 3 4 56789	1 2 3 4 56789	1 2 3 4 56789	1 2 3 4 56789	1 2 3 4 56789	1 2 3 4 56789	1 2 3 4 56789
1 2 3 4 56789	1 2 3 4 56789	1 2 3 4 56789	1 2 3 4 56789	1 2 3 4 56789	1 2 3 4 56789	1 2 3 4 56789	1 2 3 4 56789	1 2 3 4 56789
1 2 3 4 56789	1 2 3 4 56789	1 2 3 4 56789	1 2 3 4 56789	1 2 3 4 56789	1 2 3 4 56789	1 2 3 4 56789	1 2 3 4 56789	1 2 3 4 56789
1 2 3 4 56789	1 2 3 4 56789	1 2 3 4 56789	1 2 3 4 56789	1 2 3 4 56789	1 2 3 4 56789	1 2 3 4 56789	1 2 3 4 56789	1 2 3 4 56789
1 2 3 4 56789	1 2 3 4 56789	1 2 3 4 56789	1 2 3 4 56789	1 2 3 4 56789	1 2 3 4 56789	1 2 3 4 56789	1 2 3 4 56789	1 2 3 4 56789
1 2 3 4 56789	1 2 3 4 56789	1 2 3 4 56789	1 2 3 4 56789	1 2 3 4 56789	1 2 3 4 56789	1 2 3 4 56789	1 2 3 4 56789	1 2 3 4 56789
1 2 3 4 56789	1 2 3 4 56789	1 2 3 4 56789	1 2 3 4 56789	1 2 3 4 56789	1 2 3 4 56789	1 2 3 4 56789	1 2 3 4 56789	1 2 3 4 56789
1 2 3 4 56789	1 2 3 4 56789	1 2 3 4 56789	1 2 3 4 56789	1 2 3 4 56789	1 2 3 4 56789	1 2 3 4 56789	1 2 3 4 56789	1 2 3 4 56789

1234 56789	1234 56789	1234 56789	1234 56789	1234 56789	1234 56789	1234 56789	1234 56789	1234 56789
1234 56789	1234 56789	1234 56789	1234 56789	1234 56789	1234 56789	1234 56789	1234 56789	1234 56789
1234 56789	1234 56789	1234 56789	1234 56789	1234 56789	1234 56789	1234 56789	1234 56789	1234 56789
1234 56789	1234 56789	1234 56789	1234 56789	1234 56789	1234 56789	1234 56789	1234 56789	1234 56789
1234 56789	1234 56789	1234 56789	1234 56789	1234 56789	1234 56789	1234 56789	1234 56789	1234 56789
1234 56789	1234 56789	1234 56789	1234 56789	1234 56789	1234 56789	1234 56789	1234 56789	1234 56789
1234 56789	1234 56789	1234 56789	1234 56789	1234 56789	1234 56789	1234 56789	1234 56789	1234 56789
1234 56789	1234 56789	1234 56789	1234 56789	1234 56789	1234 56789	1234 56789	1234 56789	1234 56789
1234 56789	1234 56789	1234 56789	1234 56789	1234 56789	1234 56789	1234 56789	1234 56789	1234 56789

1 2 3 4 56789	1 2 3 4 56789	1 2 3 4 56789	1 2 3 4 56789	1 2 3 4 56789	1 2 3 4 56789	1 2 3 4 56789	1 2 3 4 56789	1 2 3 4 56789
1 2 3 4 56789	1 2 3 4 56789	1 2 3 4 56789	1 2 3 4 56789	1 2 3 4 56789	1 2 3 4 56789	1 2 3 4 56789	1 2 3 4 56789	1 2 3 4 56789
1 2 3 4 56789	1 2 3 4 56789	1 2 3 4 56789	1 2 3 4 56789	1 2 3 4 56789	1 2 3 4 56789	1 2 3 4 56789	1 2 3 4 56789	1 2 3 4 56789
1 2 3 4 56789	1 2 3 4 56789	1 2 3 4 56789	1 2 3 4 56789	1 2 3 4 56789	1 2 3 4 56789	1 2 3 4 56789	1 2 3 4 56789	1 2 3 4 56789
1 2 3 4 56789	1 2 3 4 56789	1 2 3 4 56789	1 2 3 4 56789	1 2 3 4 56789	1 2 3 4 56789	1 2 3 4 56789	1 2 3 4 56789	1 2 3 4 56789
1 2 3 4 56789	1 2 3 4 56789	1 2 3 4 56789	1 2 3 4 56789	1 2 3 4 56789	1 2 3 4 56789	1 2 3 4 56789	1 2 3 4 56789	1 2 3 4 56789
1 2 3 4 56789	1 2 3 4 56789	1 2 3 4 56789	1 2 3 4 56789	1 2 3 4 56789	1 2 3 4 56789	1 2 3 4 56789	1 2 3 4 56789	1 2 3 4 56789
1 2 3 4 56789	1 2 3 4 56789	1 2 3 4 56789	1 2 3 4 56789	1 2 3 4 56789	1 2 3 4 56789	1 2 3 4 56789	1 2 3 4 56789	1 2 3 4 56789
1 2 3 4 56789	1 2 3 4 56789	1 2 3 4 56789	1 2 3 4 56789	1 2 3 4 56789	1 2 3 4 56789	1 2 3 4 56789	1 2 3 4 56789	1 2 3 4 56789

1 2 3 4 56789	1 2 3 4 56789	1 2 3 4 56789	1 2 3 4 56789	1 2 3 4 56789	1 2 3 4 56789	1 2 3 4 56789	1 2 3 4 56789	1 2 3 4 56789
1 2 3 4 56789	1 2 3 4 56789	1 2 3 4 56789	1 2 3 4 56789	1 2 3 4 56789	1 2 3 4 56789	1 2 3 4 56789	1 2 3 4 56789	1 2 3 4 56789
1 2 3 4 56789	1 2 3 4 56789	1 2 3 4 56789	1 2 3 4 56789	1 2 3 4 56789	1 2 3 4 56789	1 2 3 4 56789	1 2 3 4 56789	1 2 3 4 56789
1 2 3 4 56789	1 2 3 4 56789	1 2 3 4 56789	1 2 3 4 56789	1 2 3 4 56789	1 2 3 4 56789	1 2 3 4 56789	1 2 3 4 56789	1 2 3 4 56789
1 2 3 4 56789	1 2 3 4 56789	1 2 3 4 56789	1 2 3 4 56789	1 2 3 4 56789	1 2 3 4 56789	1 2 3 4 56789	1 2 3 4 56789	1 2 3 4 56789
1 2 3 4 56789	1 2 3 4 56789	1 2 3 4 56789	1 2 3 4 56789	1 2 3 4 56789	1 2 3 4 56789	1 2 3 4 56789	1 2 3 4 56789	1 2 3 4 56789
1 2 3 4 56789	1 2 3 4 56789	1 2 3 4 56789	1 2 3 4 56789	1 2 3 4 56789	1 2 3 4 56789	1 2 3 4 56789	1 2 3 4 56789	1 2 3 4 56789
1 2 3 4 56789	1 2 3 4 56789	1 2 3 4 56789	1 2 3 4 56789	1 2 3 4 56789	1 2 3 4 56789	1 2 3 4 56789	1 2 3 4 56789	1 2 3 4 56789
1 2 3 4 56789	1 2 3 4 56789	1 2 3 4 56789	1 2 3 4 56789	1 2 3 4 56789	1 2 3 4 56789	1 2 3 4 56789	1 2 3 4 56789	1 2 3 4 56789

1 2 3 4 56789	1 2 3 4 56789	1 2 3 4 56789	1 2 3 4 56789	1 2 3 4 56789	1 2 3 4 56789	1 2 3 4 56789	1 2 3 4 56789	1 2 3 4 56789
1 2 3 4 56789	1 2 3 4 56789	1 2 3 4 56789	1 2 3 4 56789	1 2 3 4 56789	1 2 3 4 56789	1 2 3 4 56789	1 2 3 4 56789	1 2 3 4 56789
1 2 3 4 56789	1 2 3 4 56789	1 2 3 4 56789	1 2 3 4 56789	1 2 3 4 56789	1 2 3 4 56789	1 2 3 4 56789	1 2 3 4 56789	1 2 3 4 56789
1 2 3 4 56789	1 2 3 4 56789	1 2 3 4 56789	1 2 3 4 56789	1 2 3 4 56789	1 2 3 4 56789	1 2 3 4 56789	1 2 3 4 56789	1 2 3 4 56789
1 2 3 4 56789	1 2 3 4 56789	1 2 3 4 56789	1 2 3 4 56789	1 2 3 4 56789	1 2 3 4 56789	1 2 3 4 56789	1 2 3 4 56789	1 2 3 4 56789
1 2 3 4 56789	1 2 3 4 56789	1 2 3 4 56789	1 2 3 4 56789	1 2 3 4 56789	1 2 3 4 56789	1 2 3 4 56789	1 2 3 4 56789	1 2 3 4 56789
1 2 3 4 56789	1 2 3 4 56789	1 2 3 4 56789	1 2 3 4 56789	1 2 3 4 56789	1 2 3 4 56789	1 2 3 4 56789	1 2 3 4 56789	1 2 3 4 56789
1 2 3 4 56789	1 2 3 4 56789	1 2 3 4 56789	1 2 3 4 56789	1 2 3 4 56789	1 2 3 4 56789	1 2 3 4 56789	1 2 3 4 56789	1 2 3 4 56789
1 2 3 4 56789	1 2 3 4 56789	1 2 3 4 56789	1 2 3 4 56789	1 2 3 4 56789	1 2 3 4 56789	1 2 3 4 56789	1 2 3 4 56789	1 2 3 4 56789

1 2 3 4 56789	1 2 3 4 56789	1 2 3 4 56789	1 2 3 4 56789	1 2 3 4 56789	1 2 3 4 56789	1 2 3 4 56789	1 2 3 4 56789	1 2 3 4 56789
1 2 3 4 56789	1 2 3 4 56789	1 2 3 4 56789	1 2 3 4 56789	1 2 3 4 56789	1 2 3 4 56789	1 2 3 4 56789	1 2 3 4 56789	1 2 3 4 56789
1 2 3 4 56789	1 2 3 4 56789	1 2 3 4 56789	1 2 3 4 56789	1 2 3 4 56789	1 2 3 4 56789	1 2 3 4 56789	1 2 3 4 56789	1 2 3 4 56789
1 2 3 4 56789	1 2 3 4 56789	1 2 3 4 56789	1 2 3 4 56789	1 2 3 4 56789	1 2 3 4 56789	1 2 3 4 56789	1 2 3 4 56789	1 2 3 4 56789
1 2 3 4 56789	1 2 3 4 56789	1 2 3 4 56789	1 2 3 4 56789	1 2 3 4 56789	1 2 3 4 56789	1 2 3 4 56789	1 2 3 4 56789	1 2 3 4 56789
1 2 3 4 56789	1 2 3 4 56789	1 2 3 4 56789	1 2 3 4 56789	1 2 3 4 56789	1 2 3 4 56789	1 2 3 4 56789	1 2 3 4 56789	1 2 3 4 56789
1 2 3 4 56789	1 2 3 4 56789	1 2 3 4 56789	1 2 3 4 56789	1 2 3 4 56789	1 2 3 4 56789	1 2 3 4 56789	1 2 3 4 56789	1 2 3 4 56789
1 2 3 4 56789	1 2 3 4 56789	1 2 3 4 56789	1 2 3 4 56789	1 2 3 4 56789	1 2 3 4 56789	1 2 3 4 56789	1 2 3 4 56789	1 2 3 4 56789
1 2 3 4 56789	1 2 3 4 56789	1 2 3 4 56789	1 2 3 4 56789	1 2 3 4 56789	1 2 3 4 56789	1 2 3 4 56789	1 2 3 4 56789	1 2 3 4 56789

1 2 3 4 56789	1 2 3 4 56789	1 2 3 4 56789	1 2 3 4 56789	1 2 3 4 56789	1 2 3 4 56789	1 2 3 4 56789	1 2 3 4 56789	1 2 3 4 56789
1 2 3 4 56789	1 2 3 4 56789	1 2 3 4 56789	1 2 3 4 56789	1 2 3 4 56789	1 2 3 4 56789	1 2 3 4 56789	1 2 3 4 56789	1 2 3 4 56789
1 2 3 4 56789	1 2 3 4 56789	1 2 3 4 56789	1 2 3 4 56789	1 2 3 4 56789	1 2 3 4 56789	1 2 3 4 56789	1 2 3 4 56789	1 2 3 4 56789
1 2 3 4 56789	1 2 3 4 56789	1 2 3 4 56789	1 2 3 4 56789	1 2 3 4 56789	1 2 3 4 56789	1 2 3 4 56789	1 2 3 4 56789	1 2 3 4 56789
1 2 3 4 56789	1 2 3 4 56789	1 2 3 4 56789	1 2 3 4 56789	1 2 3 4 56789	1 2 3 4 56789	1 2 3 4 56789	1 2 3 4 56789	1 2 3 4 56789
1 2 3 4 56789	1 2 3 4 56789	1 2 3 4 56789	1 2 3 4 56789	1 2 3 4 56789	1 2 3 4 56789	1 2 3 4 56789	1 2 3 4 56789	1 2 3 4 56789
1 2 3 4 56789	1 2 3 4 56789	1 2 3 4 56789	1 2 3 4 56789	1 2 3 4 56789	1 2 3 4 56789	1 2 3 4 56789	1 2 3 4 56789	1 2 3 4 56789
1 2 3 4 56789	1 2 3 4 56789	1 2 3 4 56789	1 2 3 4 56789	1 2 3 4 56789	1 2 3 4 56789	1 2 3 4 56789	1 2 3 4 56789	1 2 3 4 56789
1 2 3 4 56789	1 2 3 4 56789	1 2 3 4 56789	1 2 3 4 56789	1 2 3 4 56789	1 2 3 4 56789	1 2 3 4 56789	1 2 3 4 56789	1 2 3 4 56789

1 2 3 4 56789	1 2 3 4 56789	1 2 3 4 56789	1 2 3 4 56789	1 2 3 4 56789	1 2 3 4 56789	1 2 3 4 56789	1 2 3 4 56789	1 2 3 4 56789
1 2 3 4 56789	1 2 3 4 56789	1 2 3 4 56789	1 2 3 4 56789	1 2 3 4 56789	1 2 3 4 56789	1 2 3 4 56789	1 2 3 4 56789	1 2 3 4 56789
1 2 3 4 56789	1 2 3 4 56789	1 2 3 4 56789	1 2 3 4 56789	1 2 3 4 56789	1 2 3 4 56789	1 2 3 4 56789	1 2 3 4 56789	1 2 3 4 56789
1 2 3 4 56789	1 2 3 4 56789	1 2 3 4 56789	1 2 3 4 56789	1 2 3 4 56789	1 2 3 4 56789	1 2 3 4 56789	1 2 3 4 56789	1 2 3 4 56789
1 2 3 4 56789	1 2 3 4 56789	1 2 3 4 56789	1 2 3 4 56789	1 2 3 4 56789	1 2 3 4 56789	1 2 3 4 56789	1 2 3 4 56789	1 2 3 4 56789
1 2 3 4 56789	1 2 3 4 56789	1 2 3 4 56789	1 2 3 4 56789	1 2 3 4 56789	1 2 3 4 56789	1 2 3 4 56789	1 2 3 4 56789	1 2 3 4 56789
1 2 3 4 56789	1 2 3 4 56789	1 2 3 4 56789	1 2 3 4 56789	1 2 3 4 56789	1 2 3 4 56789	1 2 3 4 56789	1 2 3 4 56789	1 2 3 4 56789
1 2 3 4 56789	1 2 3 4 56789	1 2 3 4 56789	1 2 3 4 56789	1 2 3 4 56789	1 2 3 4 56789	1 2 3 4 56789	1 2 3 4 56789	1 2 3 4 56789
1 2 3 4 56789	1 2 3 4 56789	1 2 3 4 56789	1 2 3 4 56789	1 2 3 4 56789	1 2 3 4 56789	1 2 3 4 56789	1 2 3 4 56789	1 2 3 4 56789

1 2 3 4 56789	1 2 3 4 56789	1 2 3 4 56789	1 2 3 4 56789	1 2 3 4 56789	1 2 3 4 56789	1 2 3 4 56789	1 2 3 4 56789	1 2 3 4 56789
1 2 3 4 56789	1 2 3 4 56789	1 2 3 4 56789	1 2 3 4 56789	1 2 3 4 56789	1 2 3 4 56789	1 2 3 4 56789	1 2 3 4 56789	1 2 3 4 56789
1 2 3 4 56789	1 2 3 4 56789	1 2 3 4 56789	1 2 3 4 56789	1 2 3 4 56789	1 2 3 4 56789	1 2 3 4 56789	1 2 3 4 56789	1 2 3 4 56789
1 2 3 4 56789	1 2 3 4 56789	1 2 3 4 56789	1 2 3 4 56789	1 2 3 4 56789	1 2 3 4 56789	1 2 3 4 56789	1 2 3 4 56789	1 2 3 4 56789
1 2 3 4 56789	1 2 3 4 56789	1 2 3 4 56789	1 2 3 4 56789	1 2 3 4 56789	1 2 3 4 56789	1 2 3 4 56789	1 2 3 4 56789	1 2 3 4 56789
1 2 3 4 56789	1 2 3 4 56789	1 2 3 4 56789	1 2 3 4 56789	1 2 3 4 56789	1 2 3 4 56789	1 2 3 4 56789	1 2 3 4 56789	1 2 3 4 56789
1 2 3 4 56789	1 2 3 4 56789	1 2 3 4 56789	1 2 3 4 56789	1 2 3 4 56789	1 2 3 4 56789	1 2 3 4 56789	1 2 3 4 56789	1 2 3 4 56789
1 2 3 4 56789	1 2 3 4 56789	1 2 3 4 56789	1 2 3 4 56789	1 2 3 4 56789	1 2 3 4 56789	1 2 3 4 56789	1 2 3 4 56789	1 2 3 4 56789
1 2 3 4 56789	1 2 3 4 56789	1 2 3 4 56789	1 2 3 4 56789	1 2 3 4 56789	1 2 3 4 56789	1 2 3 4 56789	1 2 3 4 56789	1 2 3 4 56789

1 2 3 4 56789	1 2 3 4 56789	1 2 3 4 56789	1 2 3 4 56789	1 2 3 4 56789	1 2 3 4 56789	1 2 3 4 56789	1 2 3 4 56789	1 2 3 4 56789
1 2 3 4 56789	1 2 3 4 56789	1 2 3 4 56789	1 2 3 4 56789	1 2 3 4 56789	1 2 3 4 56789	1 2 3 4 56789	1 2 3 4 56789	1 2 3 4 56789
1 2 3 4 56789	1 2 3 4 56789	1 2 3 4 56789	1 2 3 4 56789	1 2 3 4 56789	1 2 3 4 56789	1 2 3 4 56789	1 2 3 4 56789	1 2 3 4 56789
1 2 3 4 56789	1 2 3 4 56789	1 2 3 4 56789	1 2 3 4 56789	1 2 3 4 56789	1 2 3 4 56789	1 2 3 4 56789	1 2 3 4 56789	1 2 3 4 56789
1 2 3 4 56789	1 2 3 4 56789	1 2 3 4 56789	1 2 3 4 56789	1 2 3 4 56789	1 2 3 4 56789	1 2 3 4 56789	1 2 3 4 56789	1 2 3 4 56789
1 2 3 4 56789	1 2 3 4 56789	1 2 3 4 56789	1 2 3 4 56789	1 2 3 4 56789	1 2 3 4 56789	1 2 3 4 56789	1 2 3 4 56789	1 2 3 4 56789
1 2 3 4 56789	1 2 3 4 56789	1 2 3 4 56789	1 2 3 4 56789	1 2 3 4 56789	1 2 3 4 56789	1 2 3 4 56789	1 2 3 4 56789	1 2 3 4 56789
1 2 3 4 56789	1 2 3 4 56789	1 2 3 4 56789	1 2 3 4 56789	1 2 3 4 56789	1 2 3 4 56789	1 2 3 4 56789	1 2 3 4 56789	1 2 3 4 56789
1 2 3 4 56789	1 2 3 4 56789	1 2 3 4 56789	1 2 3 4 56789	1 2 3 4 56789	1 2 3 4 56789	1 2 3 4 56789	1 2 3 4 56789	1 2 3 4 56789

1 2 3 4 56789	1 2 3 4 56789	1 2 3 4 56789	1 2 3 4 56789	1 2 3 4 56789	1 2 3 4 56789	1 2 3 4 56789	1 2 3 4 56789	1 2 3 4 56789
1 2 3 4 56789	1 2 3 4 56789	1 2 3 4 56789	1 2 3 4 56789	1 2 3 4 56789	1 2 3 4 56789	1 2 3 4 56789	1 2 3 4 56789	1 2 3 4 56789
1 2 3 4 56789	1 2 3 4 56789	1 2 3 4 56789	1 2 3 4 56789	1 2 3 4 56789	1 2 3 4 56789	1 2 3 4 56789	1 2 3 4 56789	1 2 3 4 56789
1 2 3 4 56789	1 2 3 4 56789	1 2 3 4 56789	1 2 3 4 56789	1 2 3 4 56789	1 2 3 4 56789	1 2 3 4 56789	1 2 3 4 56789	1 2 3 4 56789
1 2 3 4 56789	1 2 3 4 56789	1 2 3 4 56789	1 2 3 4 56789	1 2 3 4 56789	1 2 3 4 56789	1 2 3 4 56789	1 2 3 4 56789	1 2 3 4 56789
1 2 3 4 56789	1 2 3 4 56789	1 2 3 4 56789	1 2 3 4 56789	1 2 3 4 56789	1 2 3 4 56789	1 2 3 4 56789	1 2 3 4 56789	1 2 3 4 56789
1 2 3 4 56789	1 2 3 4 56789	1 2 3 4 56789	1 2 3 4 56789	1 2 3 4 56789	1 2 3 4 56789	1 2 3 4 56789	1 2 3 4 56789	1 2 3 4 56789
1 2 3 4 56789	1 2 3 4 56789	1 2 3 4 56789	1 2 3 4 56789	1 2 3 4 56789	1 2 3 4 56789	1 2 3 4 56789	1 2 3 4 56789	1 2 3 4 56789
1 2 3 4 56789	1 2 3 4 56789	1 2 3 4 56789	1 2 3 4 56789	1 2 3 4 56789	1 2 3 4 56789	1 2 3 4 56789	1 2 3 4 56789	1 2 3 4 56789

1 2 3 4 56789	1 2 3 4 56789	1 2 3 4 56789	1 2 3 4 56789	1 2 3 4 56789	1 2 3 4 56789	1 2 3 4 56789	1 2 3 4 56789	1 2 3 4 56789
1 2 3 4 56789	1 2 3 4 56789	1 2 3 4 56789	1 2 3 4 56789	1 2 3 4 56789	1 2 3 4 56789	1 2 3 4 56789	1 2 3 4 56789	1 2 3 4 56789
1 2 3 4 56789	1 2 3 4 56789	1 2 3 4 56789	1 2 3 4 56789	1 2 3 4 56789	1 2 3 4 56789	1 2 3 4 56789	1 2 3 4 56789	1 2 3 4 56789
1 2 3 4 56789	1 2 3 4 56789	1 2 3 4 56789	1 2 3 4 56789	1 2 3 4 56789	1 2 3 4 56789	1 2 3 4 56789	1 2 3 4 56789	1 2 3 4 56789
1 2 3 4 56789	1 2 3 4 56789	1 2 3 4 56789	1 2 3 4 56789	1 2 3 4 56789	1 2 3 4 56789	1 2 3 4 56789	1 2 3 4 56789	1 2 3 4 56789
1 2 3 4 56789	1 2 3 4 56789	1 2 3 4 56789	1 2 3 4 56789	1 2 3 4 56789	1 2 3 4 56789	1 2 3 4 56789	1 2 3 4 56789	1 2 3 4 56789
1 2 3 4 56789	1 2 3 4 56789	1 2 3 4 56789	1 2 3 4 56789	1 2 3 4 56789	1 2 3 4 56789	1 2 3 4 56789	1 2 3 4 56789	1 2 3 4 56789
1 2 3 4 56789	1 2 3 4 56789	1 2 3 4 56789	1 2 3 4 56789	1 2 3 4 56789	1 2 3 4 56789	1 2 3 4 56789	1 2 3 4 56789	1 2 3 4 56789
1 2 3 4 56789	1 2 3 4 56789	1 2 3 4 56789	1 2 3 4 56789	1 2 3 4 56789	1 2 3 4 56789	1 2 3 4 56789	1 2 3 4 56789	1 2 3 4 56789

1 2 3 4 56789	1 2 3 4 56789	1 2 3 4 56789	1 2 3 4 56789	1 2 3 4 56789	1 2 3 4 56789	1 2 3 4 56789	1 2 3 4 56789	1 2 3 4 56789
1 2 3 4 56789	1 2 3 4 56789	1 2 3 4 56789	1 2 3 4 56789	1 2 3 4 56789	1 2 3 4 56789	1 2 3 4 56789	1 2 3 4 56789	1 2 3 4 56789
1 2 3 4 56789	1 2 3 4 56789	1 2 3 4 56789	1 2 3 4 56789	1 2 3 4 56789	1 2 3 4 56789	1 2 3 4 56789	1 2 3 4 56789	1 2 3 4 56789
1 2 3 4 56789	1 2 3 4 56789	1 2 3 4 56789	1 2 3 4 56789	1 2 3 4 56789	1 2 3 4 56789	1 2 3 4 56789	1 2 3 4 56789	1 2 3 4 56789
1 2 3 4 56789	1 2 3 4 56789	1 2 3 4 56789	1 2 3 4 56789	1 2 3 4 56789	1 2 3 4 56789	1 2 3 4 56789	1 2 3 4 56789	1 2 3 4 56789
1 2 3 4 56789	1 2 3 4 56789	1 2 3 4 56789	1 2 3 4 56789	1 2 3 4 56789	1 2 3 4 56789	1 2 3 4 56789	1 2 3 4 56789	1 2 3 4 56789
1 2 3 4 56789	1 2 3 4 56789	1 2 3 4 56789	1 2 3 4 56789	1 2 3 4 56789	1 2 3 4 56789	1 2 3 4 56789	1 2 3 4 56789	1 2 3 4 56789
1 2 3 4 56789	1 2 3 4 56789	1 2 3 4 56789	1 2 3 4 56789	1 2 3 4 56789	1 2 3 4 56789	1 2 3 4 56789	1 2 3 4 56789	1 2 3 4 56789
1 2 3 4 56789	1 2 3 4 56789	1 2 3 4 56789	1 2 3 4 56789	1 2 3 4 56789	1 2 3 4 56789	1 2 3 4 56789	1 2 3 4 56789	1 2 3 4 56789

1 2 3 4 56789	1 2 3 4 56789	1 2 3 4 56789	1 2 3 4 56789	1 2 3 4 56789	1 2 3 4 56789	1 2 3 4 56789	1 2 3 4 56789	1 2 3 4 56789
1 2 3 4 56789	1 2 3 4 56789	1 2 3 4 56789	1 2 3 4 56789	1 2 3 4 56789	1 2 3 4 56789	1 2 3 4 56789	1 2 3 4 56789	1 2 3 4 56789
1 2 3 4 56789	1 2 3 4 56789	1 2 3 4 56789	1 2 3 4 56789	1 2 3 4 56789	1 2 3 4 56789	1 2 3 4 56789	1 2 3 4 56789	1 2 3 4 56789
1 2 3 4 56789	1 2 3 4 56789	1 2 3 4 56789	1 2 3 4 56789	1 2 3 4 56789	1 2 3 4 56789	1 2 3 4 56789	1 2 3 4 56789	1 2 3 4 56789
1 2 3 4 56789	1 2 3 4 56789	1 2 3 4 56789	1 2 3 4 56789	1 2 3 4 56789	1 2 3 4 56789	1 2 3 4 56789	1 2 3 4 56789	1 2 3 4 56789
1 2 3 4 56789	1 2 3 4 56789	1 2 3 4 56789	1 2 3 4 56789	1 2 3 4 56789	1 2 3 4 56789	1 2 3 4 56789	1 2 3 4 56789	1 2 3 4 56789
1 2 3 4 56789	1 2 3 4 56789	1 2 3 4 56789	1 2 3 4 56789	1 2 3 4 56789	1 2 3 4 56789	1 2 3 4 56789	1 2 3 4 56789	1 2 3 4 56789
1 2 3 4 56789	1 2 3 4 56789	1 2 3 4 56789	1 2 3 4 56789	1 2 3 4 56789	1 2 3 4 56789	1 2 3 4 56789	1 2 3 4 56789	1 2 3 4 56789
1 2 3 4 56789	1 2 3 4 56789	1 2 3 4 56789	1 2 3 4 56789	1 2 3 4 56789	1 2 3 4 56789	1 2 3 4 56789	1 2 3 4 56789	1 2 3 4 56789

1 2 3 4 56789	1 2 3 4 56789	1 2 3 4 56789	1 2 3 4 56789	1 2 3 4 56789	1 2 3 4 56789	1 2 3 4 56789	1 2 3 4 56789	1 2 3 4 56789
1 2 3 4 56789	1 2 3 4 56789	1 2 3 4 56789	1 2 3 4 56789	1 2 3 4 56789	1 2 3 4 56789	1 2 3 4 56789	1 2 3 4 56789	1 2 3 4 56789
1 2 3 4 56789	1 2 3 4 56789	1 2 3 4 56789	1 2 3 4 56789	1 2 3 4 56789	1 2 3 4 56789	1 2 3 4 56789	1 2 3 4 56789	1 2 3 4 56789
1 2 3 4 56789	1 2 3 4 56789	1 2 3 4 56789	1 2 3 4 56789	1 2 3 4 56789	1 2 3 4 56789	1 2 3 4 56789	1 2 3 4 56789	1 2 3 4 56789
1 2 3 4 56789	1 2 3 4 56789	1 2 3 4 56789	1 2 3 4 56789	1 2 3 4 56789	1 2 3 4 56789	1 2 3 4 56789	1 2 3 4 56789	1 2 3 4 56789
1 2 3 4 56789	1 2 3 4 56789	1 2 3 4 56789	1 2 3 4 56789	1 2 3 4 56789	1 2 3 4 56789	1 2 3 4 56789	1 2 3 4 56789	1 2 3 4 56789
1 2 3 4 56789	1 2 3 4 56789	1 2 3 4 56789	1 2 3 4 56789	1 2 3 4 56789	1 2 3 4 56789	1 2 3 4 56789	1 2 3 4 56789	1 2 3 4 56789
1 2 3 4 56789	1 2 3 4 56789	1 2 3 4 56789	1 2 3 4 56789	1 2 3 4 56789	1 2 3 4 56789	1 2 3 4 56789	1 2 3 4 56789	1 2 3 4 56789
1 2 3 4 56789	1 2 3 4 56789	1 2 3 4 56789	1 2 3 4 56789	1 2 3 4 56789	1 2 3 4 56789	1 2 3 4 56789	1 2 3 4 56789	1 2 3 4 56789

1234 56789	1234 56789	1234 56789	1234 56789	1234 56789	1234 56789	1234 56789	1234 56789	1234 56789
1234 56789	1234 56789	1234 56789	1234 56789	1234 56789	1234 56789	1234 56789	1234 56789	1234 56789
1234 56789	1234 56789	1234 56789	1234 56789	1234 56789	1234 56789	1234 56789	1234 56789	1234 56789
1234 56789	1234 56789	1234 56789	1234 56789	1234 56789	1234 56789	1234 56789	1234 56789	1234 56789
1234 56789	1234 56789	1234 56789	1234 56789	1234 56789	1234 56789	1234 56789	1234 56789	1234 56789
1234 56789	1234 56789	1234 56789	1234 56789	1234 56789	1234 56789	1234 56789	1234 56789	1234 56789
1234 56789	1234 56789	1234 56789	1234 56789	1234 56789	1234 56789	1234 56789	1234 56789	1234 56789
1234 56789	1234 56789	1234 56789	1234 56789	1234 56789	1234 56789	1234 56789	1234 56789	1234 56789
1234 56789	1234 56789	1234 56789	1234 56789	1234 56789	1234 56789	1234 56789	1234 56789	1234 56789

1 2 3 4 56789	1 2 3 4 56789	1 2 3 4 56789	1 2 3 4 56789	1 2 3 4 56789	1 2 3 4 56789	1 2 3 4 56789	1 2 3 4 56789	1 2 3 4 56789
1 2 3 4 56789	1 2 3 4 56789	1 2 3 4 56789	1 2 3 4 56789	1 2 3 4 56789	1 2 3 4 56789	1 2 3 4 56789	1 2 3 4 56789	1 2 3 4 56789
1 2 3 4 56789	1 2 3 4 56789	1 2 3 4 56789	1 2 3 4 56789	1 2 3 4 56789	1 2 3 4 56789	1 2 3 4 56789	1 2 3 4 56789	1 2 3 4 56789
1 2 3 4 56789	1 2 3 4 56789	1 2 3 4 56789	1 2 3 4 56789	1 2 3 4 56789	1 2 3 4 56789	1 2 3 4 56789	1 2 3 4 56789	1 2 3 4 56789
1 2 3 4 56789	1 2 3 4 56789	1 2 3 4 56789	1 2 3 4 56789	1 2 3 4 56789	1 2 3 4 56789	1 2 3 4 56789	1 2 3 4 56789	1 2 3 4 56789
1 2 3 4 56789	1 2 3 4 56789	1 2 3 4 56789	1 2 3 4 56789	1 2 3 4 56789	1 2 3 4 56789	1 2 3 4 56789	1 2 3 4 56789	1 2 3 4 56789
1 2 3 4 56789	1 2 3 4 56789	1 2 3 4 56789	1 2 3 4 56789	1 2 3 4 56789	1 2 3 4 56789	1 2 3 4 56789	1 2 3 4 56789	1 2 3 4 56789
1 2 3 4 56789	1 2 3 4 56789	1 2 3 4 56789	1 2 3 4 56789	1 2 3 4 56789	1 2 3 4 56789	1 2 3 4 56789	1 2 3 4 56789	1 2 3 4 56789
1 2 3 4 56789	1 2 3 4 56789	1 2 3 4 56789	1 2 3 4 56789	1 2 3 4 56789	1 2 3 4 56789	1 2 3 4 56789	1 2 3 4 56789	1 2 3 4 56789

1 2 3 4 56789	1 2 3 4 56789	1 2 3 4 56789	1 2 3 4 56789	1 2 3 4 56789	1 2 3 4 56789	1 2 3 4 56789	1 2 3 4 56789	1 2 3 4 56789
1 2 3 4 56789	1 2 3 4 56789	1 2 3 4 56789	1 2 3 4 56789	1 2 3 4 56789	1 2 3 4 56789	1 2 3 4 56789	1 2 3 4 56789	1 2 3 4 56789
1 2 3 4 56789	1 2 3 4 56789	1 2 3 4 56789	1 2 3 4 56789	1 2 3 4 56789	1 2 3 4 56789	1 2 3 4 56789	1 2 3 4 56789	1 2 3 4 56789
1 2 3 4 56789	1 2 3 4 56789	1 2 3 4 56789	1 2 3 4 56789	1 2 3 4 56789	1 2 3 4 56789	1 2 3 4 56789	1 2 3 4 56789	1 2 3 4 56789
1 2 3 4 56789	1 2 3 4 56789	1 2 3 4 56789	1 2 3 4 56789	1 2 3 4 56789	1 2 3 4 56789	1 2 3 4 56789	1 2 3 4 56789	1 2 3 4 56789
1 2 3 4 56789	1 2 3 4 56789	1 2 3 4 56789	1 2 3 4 56789	1 2 3 4 56789	1 2 3 4 56789	1 2 3 4 56789	1 2 3 4 56789	1 2 3 4 56789
1 2 3 4 56789	1 2 3 4 56789	1 2 3 4 56789	1 2 3 4 56789	1 2 3 4 56789	1 2 3 4 56789	1 2 3 4 56789	1 2 3 4 56789	1 2 3 4 56789
1 2 3 4 56789	1 2 3 4 56789	1 2 3 4 56789	1 2 3 4 56789	1 2 3 4 56789	1 2 3 4 56789	1 2 3 4 56789	1 2 3 4 56789	1 2 3 4 56789
1 2 3 4 56789	1 2 3 4 56789	1 2 3 4 56789	1 2 3 4 56789	1 2 3 4 56789	1 2 3 4 56789	1 2 3 4 56789	1 2 3 4 56789	1 2 3 4 56789

1 2 3 4 56789	1 2 3 4 56789	1 2 3 4 56789	1 2 3 4 56789	1 2 3 4 56789	1 2 3 4 56789	1 2 3 4 56789	1 2 3 4 56789	1 2 3 4 56789
1 2 3 4 56789	1 2 3 4 56789	1 2 3 4 56789	1 2 3 4 56789	1 2 3 4 56789	1 2 3 4 56789	1 2 3 4 56789	1 2 3 4 56789	1 2 3 4 56789
1 2 3 4 56789	1 2 3 4 56789	1 2 3 4 56789	1 2 3 4 56789	1 2 3 4 56789	1 2 3 4 56789	1 2 3 4 56789	1 2 3 4 56789	1 2 3 4 56789
1 2 3 4 56789	1 2 3 4 56789	1 2 3 4 56789	1 2 3 4 56789	1 2 3 4 56789	1 2 3 4 56789	1 2 3 4 56789	1 2 3 4 56789	1 2 3 4 56789
1 2 3 4 56789	1 2 3 4 56789	1 2 3 4 56789	1 2 3 4 56789	1 2 3 4 56789	1 2 3 4 56789	1 2 3 4 56789	1 2 3 4 56789	1 2 3 4 56789
1 2 3 4 56789	1 2 3 4 56789	1 2 3 4 56789	1 2 3 4 56789	1 2 3 4 56789	1 2 3 4 56789	1 2 3 4 56789	1 2 3 4 56789	1 2 3 4 56789
1 2 3 4 56789	1 2 3 4 56789	1 2 3 4 56789	1 2 3 4 56789	1 2 3 4 56789	1 2 3 4 56789	1 2 3 4 56789	1 2 3 4 56789	1 2 3 4 56789
1 2 3 4 56789	1 2 3 4 56789	1 2 3 4 56789	1 2 3 4 56789	1 2 3 4 56789	1 2 3 4 56789	1 2 3 4 56789	1 2 3 4 56789	1 2 3 4 56789
1 2 3 4 56789	1 2 3 4 56789	1 2 3 4 56789	1 2 3 4 56789	1 2 3 4 56789	1 2 3 4 56789	1 2 3 4 56789	1 2 3 4 56789	1 2 3 4 56789

1 2 3 4 56789	1 2 3 4 56789	1 2 3 4 56789	1 2 3 4 56789	1 2 3 4 56789	1 2 3 4 56789	1 2 3 4 56789	1 2 3 4 56789	1 2 3 4 56789
1 2 3 4 56789	1 2 3 4 56789	1 2 3 4 56789	1 2 3 4 56789	1 2 3 4 56789	1 2 3 4 56789	1 2 3 4 56789	1 2 3 4 56789	1 2 3 4 56789
1 2 3 4 56789	1 2 3 4 56789	1 2 3 4 56789	1 2 3 4 56789	1 2 3 4 56789	1 2 3 4 56789	1 2 3 4 56789	1 2 3 4 56789	1 2 3 4 56789
1 2 3 4 56789	1 2 3 4 56789	1 2 3 4 56789	1 2 3 4 56789	1 2 3 4 56789	1 2 3 4 56789	1 2 3 4 56789	1 2 3 4 56789	1 2 3 4 56789
1 2 3 4 56789	1 2 3 4 56789	1 2 3 4 56789	1 2 3 4 56789	1 2 3 4 56789	1 2 3 4 56789	1 2 3 4 56789	1 2 3 4 56789	1 2 3 4 56789
1 2 3 4 56789	1 2 3 4 56789	1 2 3 4 56789	1 2 3 4 56789	1 2 3 4 56789	1 2 3 4 56789	1 2 3 4 56789	1 2 3 4 56789	1 2 3 4 56789
1 2 3 4 56789	1 2 3 4 56789	1 2 3 4 56789	1 2 3 4 56789	1 2 3 4 56789	1 2 3 4 56789	1 2 3 4 56789	1 2 3 4 56789	1 2 3 4 56789
1 2 3 4 56789	1 2 3 4 56789	1 2 3 4 56789	1 2 3 4 56789	1 2 3 4 56789	1 2 3 4 56789	1 2 3 4 56789	1 2 3 4 56789	1 2 3 4 56789
1 2 3 4 56789	1 2 3 4 56789	1 2 3 4 56789	1 2 3 4 56789	1 2 3 4 56789	1 2 3 4 56789	1 2 3 4 56789	1 2 3 4 56789	1 2 3 4 56789

1 2 3 4 56789	1 2 3 4 56789	1 2 3 4 56789	1 2 3 4 56789	1 2 3 4 56789	1 2 3 4 56789	1 2 3 4 56789	1 2 3 4 56789	1 2 3 4 56789
1 2 3 4 56789	1 2 3 4 56789	1 2 3 4 56789	1 2 3 4 56789	1 2 3 4 56789	1 2 3 4 56789	1 2 3 4 56789	1 2 3 4 56789	1 2 3 4 56789
1 2 3 4 56789	1 2 3 4 56789	1 2 3 4 56789	1 2 3 4 56789	1 2 3 4 56789	1 2 3 4 56789	1 2 3 4 56789	1 2 3 4 56789	1 2 3 4 56789
1 2 3 4 56789	1 2 3 4 56789	1 2 3 4 56789	1 2 3 4 56789	1 2 3 4 56789	1 2 3 4 56789	1 2 3 4 56789	1 2 3 4 56789	1 2 3 4 56789
1 2 3 4 56789	1 2 3 4 56789	1 2 3 4 56789	1 2 3 4 56789	1 2 3 4 56789	1 2 3 4 56789	1 2 3 4 56789	1 2 3 4 56789	1 2 3 4 56789
1 2 3 4 56789	1 2 3 4 56789	1 2 3 4 56789	1 2 3 4 56789	1 2 3 4 56789	1 2 3 4 56789	1 2 3 4 56789	1 2 3 4 56789	1 2 3 4 56789
1 2 3 4 56789	1 2 3 4 56789	1 2 3 4 56789	1 2 3 4 56789	1 2 3 4 56789	1 2 3 4 56789	1 2 3 4 56789	1 2 3 4 56789	1 2 3 4 56789
1 2 3 4 56789	1 2 3 4 56789	1 2 3 4 56789	1 2 3 4 56789	1 2 3 4 56789	1 2 3 4 56789	1 2 3 4 56789	1 2 3 4 56789	1 2 3 4 56789
1 2 3 4 56789	1 2 3 4 56789	1 2 3 4 56789	1 2 3 4 56789	1 2 3 4 56789	1 2 3 4 56789	1 2 3 4 56789	1 2 3 4 56789	1 2 3 4 56789

1 2 3 4 56789	1 2 3 4 56789	1 2 3 4 56789	1 2 3 4 56789	1 2 3 4 56789	1 2 3 4 56789	1 2 3 4 56789	1 2 3 4 56789	1 2 3 4 56789
1 2 3 4 56789	1 2 3 4 56789	1 2 3 4 56789	1 2 3 4 56789	1 2 3 4 56789	1 2 3 4 56789	1 2 3 4 56789	1 2 3 4 56789	1 2 3 4 56789
1 2 3 4 56789	1 2 3 4 56789	1 2 3 4 56789	1 2 3 4 56789	1 2 3 4 56789	1 2 3 4 56789	1 2 3 4 56789	1 2 3 4 56789	1 2 3 4 56789
1 2 3 4 56789	1 2 3 4 56789	1 2 3 4 56789	1 2 3 4 56789	1 2 3 4 56789	1 2 3 4 56789	1 2 3 4 56789	1 2 3 4 56789	1 2 3 4 56789
1 2 3 4 56789	1 2 3 4 56789	1 2 3 4 56789	1 2 3 4 56789	1 2 3 4 56789	1 2 3 4 56789	1 2 3 4 56789	1 2 3 4 56789	1 2 3 4 56789
1 2 3 4 56789	1 2 3 4 56789	1 2 3 4 56789	1 2 3 4 56789	1 2 3 4 56789	1 2 3 4 56789	1 2 3 4 56789	1 2 3 4 56789	1 2 3 4 56789
1 2 3 4 56789	1 2 3 4 56789	1 2 3 4 56789	1 2 3 4 56789	1 2 3 4 56789	1 2 3 4 56789	1 2 3 4 56789	1 2 3 4 56789	1 2 3 4 56789
1 2 3 4 56789	1 2 3 4 56789	1 2 3 4 56789	1 2 3 4 56789	1 2 3 4 56789	1 2 3 4 56789	1 2 3 4 56789	1 2 3 4 56789	1 2 3 4 56789
1 2 3 4 56789	1 2 3 4 56789	1 2 3 4 56789	1 2 3 4 56789	1 2 3 4 56789	1 2 3 4 56789	1 2 3 4 56789	1 2 3 4 56789	1 2 3 4 56789

1 2 3 4 56789	1 2 3 4 56789	1 2 3 4 56789	1 2 3 4 56789	1 2 3 4 56789	1 2 3 4 56789	1 2 3 4 56789	1 2 3 4 56789	1 2 3 4 56789
1 2 3 4 56789	1 2 3 4 56789	1 2 3 4 56789	1 2 3 4 56789	1 2 3 4 56789	1 2 3 4 56789	1 2 3 4 56789	1 2 3 4 56789	1 2 3 4 56789
1 2 3 4 56789	1 2 3 4 56789	1 2 3 4 56789	1 2 3 4 56789	1 2 3 4 56789	1 2 3 4 56789	1 2 3 4 56789	1 2 3 4 56789	1 2 3 4 56789
1 2 3 4 56789	1 2 3 4 56789	1 2 3 4 56789	1 2 3 4 56789	1 2 3 4 56789	1 2 3 4 56789	1 2 3 4 56789	1 2 3 4 56789	1 2 3 4 56789
1 2 3 4 56789	1 2 3 4 56789	1 2 3 4 56789	1 2 3 4 56789	1 2 3 4 56789	1 2 3 4 56789	1 2 3 4 56789	1 2 3 4 56789	1 2 3 4 56789
1 2 3 4 56789	1 2 3 4 56789	1 2 3 4 56789	1 2 3 4 56789	1 2 3 4 56789	1 2 3 4 56789	1 2 3 4 56789	1 2 3 4 56789	1 2 3 4 56789
1 2 3 4 56789	1 2 3 4 56789	1 2 3 4 56789	1 2 3 4 56789	1 2 3 4 56789	1 2 3 4 56789	1 2 3 4 56789	1 2 3 4 56789	1 2 3 4 56789
1 2 3 4 56789	1 2 3 4 56789	1 2 3 4 56789	1 2 3 4 56789	1 2 3 4 56789	1 2 3 4 56789	1 2 3 4 56789	1 2 3 4 56789	1 2 3 4 56789
1 2 3 4 56789	1 2 3 4 56789	1 2 3 4 56789	1 2 3 4 56789	1 2 3 4 56789	1 2 3 4 56789	1 2 3 4 56789	1 2 3 4 56789	1 2 3 4 56789

1 2 3 4 56789	1 2 3 4 56789	1 2 3 4 56789	1 2 3 4 56789	1 2 3 4 56789	1 2 3 4 56789	1 2 3 4 56789	1 2 3 4 56789	1 2 3 4 56789
1 2 3 4 56789	1 2 3 4 56789	1 2 3 4 56789	1 2 3 4 56789	1 2 3 4 56789	1 2 3 4 56789	1 2 3 4 56789	1 2 3 4 56789	1 2 3 4 56789
1 2 3 4 56789	1 2 3 4 56789	1 2 3 4 56789	1 2 3 4 56789	1 2 3 4 56789	1 2 3 4 56789	1 2 3 4 56789	1 2 3 4 56789	1 2 3 4 56789
1 2 3 4 56789	1 2 3 4 56789	1 2 3 4 56789	1 2 3 4 56789	1 2 3 4 56789	1 2 3 4 56789	1 2 3 4 56789	1 2 3 4 56789	1 2 3 4 56789
1 2 3 4 56789	1 2 3 4 56789	1 2 3 4 56789	1 2 3 4 56789	1 2 3 4 56789	1 2 3 4 56789	1 2 3 4 56789	1 2 3 4 56789	1 2 3 4 56789
1 2 3 4 56789	1 2 3 4 56789	1 2 3 4 56789	1 2 3 4 56789	1 2 3 4 56789	1 2 3 4 56789	1 2 3 4 56789	1 2 3 4 56789	1 2 3 4 56789
1 2 3 4 56789	1 2 3 4 56789	1 2 3 4 56789	1 2 3 4 56789	1 2 3 4 56789	1 2 3 4 56789	1 2 3 4 56789	1 2 3 4 56789	1 2 3 4 56789
1 2 3 4 56789	1 2 3 4 56789	1 2 3 4 56789	1 2 3 4 56789	1 2 3 4 56789	1 2 3 4 56789	1 2 3 4 56789	1 2 3 4 56789	1 2 3 4 56789
1 2 3 4 56789	1 2 3 4 56789	1 2 3 4 56789	1 2 3 4 56789	1 2 3 4 56789	1 2 3 4 56789	1 2 3 4 56789	1 2 3 4 56789	1 2 3 4 56789

1 2 3 4 56789	1 2 3 4 56789	1 2 3 4 56789	1 2 3 4 56789	1 2 3 4 56789	1 2 3 4 56789	1 2 3 4 56789	1 2 3 4 56789	1 2 3 4 56789
1 2 3 4 56789	1 2 3 4 56789	1 2 3 4 56789	1 2 3 4 56789	1 2 3 4 56789	1 2 3 4 56789	1 2 3 4 56789	1 2 3 4 56789	1 2 3 4 56789
1 2 3 4 56789	1 2 3 4 56789	1 2 3 4 56789	1 2 3 4 56789	1 2 3 4 56789	1 2 3 4 56789	1 2 3 4 56789	1 2 3 4 56789	1 2 3 4 56789
1 2 3 4 56789	1 2 3 4 56789	1 2 3 4 56789	1 2 3 4 56789	1 2 3 4 56789	1 2 3 4 56789	1 2 3 4 56789	1 2 3 4 56789	1 2 3 4 56789
1 2 3 4 56789	1 2 3 4 56789	1 2 3 4 56789	1 2 3 4 56789	1 2 3 4 56789	1 2 3 4 56789	1 2 3 4 56789	1 2 3 4 56789	1 2 3 4 56789
1 2 3 4 56789	1 2 3 4 56789	1 2 3 4 56789	1 2 3 4 56789	1 2 3 4 56789	1 2 3 4 56789	1 2 3 4 56789	1 2 3 4 56789	1 2 3 4 56789
1 2 3 4 56789	1 2 3 4 56789	1 2 3 4 56789	1 2 3 4 56789	1 2 3 4 56789	1 2 3 4 56789	1 2 3 4 56789	1 2 3 4 56789	1 2 3 4 56789
1 2 3 4 56789	1 2 3 4 56789	1 2 3 4 56789	1 2 3 4 56789	1 2 3 4 56789	1 2 3 4 56789	1 2 3 4 56789	1 2 3 4 56789	1 2 3 4 56789
1 2 3 4 56789	1 2 3 4 56789	1 2 3 4 56789	1 2 3 4 56789	1 2 3 4 56789	1 2 3 4 56789	1 2 3 4 56789	1 2 3 4 56789	1 2 3 4 56789

1 2 3 4 56789	1 2 3 4 56789	1 2 3 4 56789	1 2 3 4 56789	1 2 3 4 56789	1 2 3 4 56789	1 2 3 4 56789	1 2 3 4 56789	1 2 3 4 56789
1 2 3 4 56789	1 2 3 4 56789	1 2 3 4 56789	1 2 3 4 56789	1 2 3 4 56789	1 2 3 4 56789	1 2 3 4 56789	1 2 3 4 56789	1 2 3 4 56789
1 2 3 4 56789	1 2 3 4 56789	1 2 3 4 56789	1 2 3 4 56789	1 2 3 4 56789	1 2 3 4 56789	1 2 3 4 56789	1 2 3 4 56789	1 2 3 4 56789
1 2 3 4 56789	1 2 3 4 56789	1 2 3 4 56789	1 2 3 4 56789	1 2 3 4 56789	1 2 3 4 56789	1 2 3 4 56789	1 2 3 4 56789	1 2 3 4 56789
1 2 3 4 56789	1 2 3 4 56789	1 2 3 4 56789	1 2 3 4 56789	1 2 3 4 56789	1 2 3 4 56789	1 2 3 4 56789	1 2 3 4 56789	1 2 3 4 56789
1 2 3 4 56789	1 2 3 4 56789	1 2 3 4 56789	1 2 3 4 56789	1 2 3 4 56789	1 2 3 4 56789	1 2 3 4 56789	1 2 3 4 56789	1 2 3 4 56789
1 2 3 4 56789	1 2 3 4 56789	1 2 3 4 56789	1 2 3 4 56789	1 2 3 4 56789	1 2 3 4 56789	1 2 3 4 56789	1 2 3 4 56789	1 2 3 4 56789
1 2 3 4 56789	1 2 3 4 56789	1 2 3 4 56789	1 2 3 4 56789	1 2 3 4 56789	1 2 3 4 56789	1 2 3 4 56789	1 2 3 4 56789	1 2 3 4 56789
1 2 3 4 56789	1 2 3 4 56789	1 2 3 4 56789	1 2 3 4 56789	1 2 3 4 56789	1 2 3 4 56789	1 2 3 4 56789	1 2 3 4 56789	1 2 3 4 56789

1 2 3 4 56789	1 2 3 4 56789	1 2 3 4 56789	1 2 3 4 56789	1 2 3 4 56789	1 2 3 4 56789	1 2 3 4 56789	1 2 3 4 56789	1 2 3 4 56789
1 2 3 4 56789	1 2 3 4 56789	1 2 3 4 56789	1 2 3 4 56789	1 2 3 4 56789	1 2 3 4 56789	1 2 3 4 56789	1 2 3 4 56789	1 2 3 4 56789
1 2 3 4 56789	1 2 3 4 56789	1 2 3 4 56789	1 2 3 4 56789	1 2 3 4 56789	1 2 3 4 56789	1 2 3 4 56789	1 2 3 4 56789	1 2 3 4 56789
1 2 3 4 56789	1 2 3 4 56789	1 2 3 4 56789	1 2 3 4 56789	1 2 3 4 56789	1 2 3 4 56789	1 2 3 4 56789	1 2 3 4 56789	1 2 3 4 56789
1 2 3 4 56789	1 2 3 4 56789	1 2 3 4 56789	1 2 3 4 56789	1 2 3 4 56789	1 2 3 4 56789	1 2 3 4 56789	1 2 3 4 56789	1 2 3 4 56789
1 2 3 4 56789	1 2 3 4 56789	1 2 3 4 56789	1 2 3 4 56789	1 2 3 4 56789	1 2 3 4 56789	1 2 3 4 56789	1 2 3 4 56789	1 2 3 4 56789
1 2 3 4 56789	1 2 3 4 56789	1 2 3 4 56789	1 2 3 4 56789	1 2 3 4 56789	1 2 3 4 56789	1 2 3 4 56789	1 2 3 4 56789	1 2 3 4 56789
1 2 3 4 56789	1 2 3 4 56789	1 2 3 4 56789	1 2 3 4 56789	1 2 3 4 56789	1 2 3 4 56789	1 2 3 4 56789	1 2 3 4 56789	1 2 3 4 56789
1 2 3 4 56789	1 2 3 4 56789	1 2 3 4 56789	1 2 3 4 56789	1 2 3 4 56789	1 2 3 4 56789	1 2 3 4 56789	1 2 3 4 56789	1 2 3 4 56789

1 2 3 4 56789	1 2 3 4 56789	1 2 3 4 56789	1 2 3 4 56789	1 2 3 4 56789	1 2 3 4 56789	1 2 3 4 56789	1 2 3 4 56789	1 2 3 4 56789
1 2 3 4 56789	1 2 3 4 56789	1 2 3 4 56789	1 2 3 4 56789	1 2 3 4 56789	1 2 3 4 56789	1 2 3 4 56789	1 2 3 4 56789	1 2 3 4 56789
1 2 3 4 56789	1 2 3 4 56789	1 2 3 4 56789	1 2 3 4 56789	1 2 3 4 56789	1 2 3 4 56789	1 2 3 4 56789	1 2 3 4 56789	1 2 3 4 56789
1 2 3 4 56789	1 2 3 4 56789	1 2 3 4 56789	1 2 3 4 56789	1 2 3 4 56789	1 2 3 4 56789	1 2 3 4 56789	1 2 3 4 56789	1 2 3 4 56789
1 2 3 4 56789	1 2 3 4 56789	1 2 3 4 56789	1 2 3 4 56789	1 2 3 4 56789	1 2 3 4 56789	1 2 3 4 56789	1 2 3 4 56789	1 2 3 4 56789
1 2 3 4 56789	1 2 3 4 56789	1 2 3 4 56789	1 2 3 4 56789	1 2 3 4 56789	1 2 3 4 56789	1 2 3 4 56789	1 2 3 4 56789	1 2 3 4 56789
1 2 3 4 56789	1 2 3 4 56789	1 2 3 4 56789	1 2 3 4 56789	1 2 3 4 56789	1 2 3 4 56789	1 2 3 4 56789	1 2 3 4 56789	1 2 3 4 56789
1 2 3 4 56789	1 2 3 4 56789	1 2 3 4 56789	1 2 3 4 56789	1 2 3 4 56789	1 2 3 4 56789	1 2 3 4 56789	1 2 3 4 56789	1 2 3 4 56789
1 2 3 4 56789	1 2 3 4 56789	1 2 3 4 56789	1 2 3 4 56789	1 2 3 4 56789	1 2 3 4 56789	1 2 3 4 56789	1 2 3 4 56789	1 2 3 4 56789

1 2 3 4 56789	1 2 3 4 56789	1 2 3 4 56789	1 2 3 4 56789	1 2 3 4 56789	1 2 3 4 56789	1 2 3 4 56789	1 2 3 4 56789	1 2 3 4 56789
1 2 3 4 56789	1 2 3 4 56789	1 2 3 4 56789	1 2 3 4 56789	1 2 3 4 56789	1 2 3 4 56789	1 2 3 4 56789	1 2 3 4 56789	1 2 3 4 56789
1 2 3 4 56789	1 2 3 4 56789	1 2 3 4 56789	1 2 3 4 56789	1 2 3 4 56789	1 2 3 4 56789	1 2 3 4 56789	1 2 3 4 56789	1 2 3 4 56789
1 2 3 4 56789	1 2 3 4 56789	1 2 3 4 56789	1 2 3 4 56789	1 2 3 4 56789	1 2 3 4 56789	1 2 3 4 56789	1 2 3 4 56789	1 2 3 4 56789
1 2 3 4 56789	1 2 3 4 56789	1 2 3 4 56789	1 2 3 4 56789	1 2 3 4 56789	1 2 3 4 56789	1 2 3 4 56789	1 2 3 4 56789	1 2 3 4 56789
1 2 3 4 56789	1 2 3 4 56789	1 2 3 4 56789	1 2 3 4 56789	1 2 3 4 56789	1 2 3 4 56789	1 2 3 4 56789	1 2 3 4 56789	1 2 3 4 56789
1 2 3 4 56789	1 2 3 4 56789	1 2 3 4 56789	1 2 3 4 56789	1 2 3 4 56789	1 2 3 4 56789	1 2 3 4 56789	1 2 3 4 56789	1 2 3 4 56789
1 2 3 4 56789	1 2 3 4 56789	1 2 3 4 56789	1 2 3 4 56789	1 2 3 4 56789	1 2 3 4 56789	1 2 3 4 56789	1 2 3 4 56789	1 2 3 4 56789
1 2 3 4 56789	1 2 3 4 56789	1 2 3 4 56789	1 2 3 4 56789	1 2 3 4 56789	1 2 3 4 56789	1 2 3 4 56789	1 2 3 4 56789	1 2 3 4 56789

1 2 3 4 56789	1 2 3 4 56789	1 2 3 4 56789	1 2 3 4 56789	1 2 3 4 56789	1 2 3 4 56789	1 2 3 4 56789	1 2 3 4 56789	1 2 3 4 56789
1 2 3 4 56789	1 2 3 4 56789	1 2 3 4 56789	1 2 3 4 56789	1 2 3 4 56789	1 2 3 4 56789	1 2 3 4 56789	1 2 3 4 56789	1 2 3 4 56789
1 2 3 4 56789	1 2 3 4 56789	1 2 3 4 56789	1 2 3 4 56789	1 2 3 4 56789	1 2 3 4 56789	1 2 3 4 56789	1 2 3 4 56789	1 2 3 4 56789
1 2 3 4 56789	1 2 3 4 56789	1 2 3 4 56789	1 2 3 4 56789	1 2 3 4 56789	1 2 3 4 56789	1 2 3 4 56789	1 2 3 4 56789	1 2 3 4 56789
1 2 3 4 56789	1 2 3 4 56789	1 2 3 4 56789	1 2 3 4 56789	1 2 3 4 56789	1 2 3 4 56789	1 2 3 4 56789	1 2 3 4 56789	1 2 3 4 56789
1 2 3 4 56789	1 2 3 4 56789	1 2 3 4 56789	1 2 3 4 56789	1 2 3 4 56789	1 2 3 4 56789	1 2 3 4 56789	1 2 3 4 56789	1 2 3 4 56789
1 2 3 4 56789	1 2 3 4 56789	1 2 3 4 56789	1 2 3 4 56789	1 2 3 4 56789	1 2 3 4 56789	1 2 3 4 56789	1 2 3 4 56789	1 2 3 4 56789
1 2 3 4 56789	1 2 3 4 56789	1 2 3 4 56789	1 2 3 4 56789	1 2 3 4 56789	1 2 3 4 56789	1 2 3 4 56789	1 2 3 4 56789	1 2 3 4 56789
1 2 3 4 56789	1 2 3 4 56789	1 2 3 4 56789	1 2 3 4 56789	1 2 3 4 56789	1 2 3 4 56789	1 2 3 4 56789	1 2 3 4 56789	1 2 3 4 56789

1 2 3 4 56789	1 2 3 4 56789	1 2 3 4 56789	1 2 3 4 56789	1 2 3 4 56789	1 2 3 4 56789	1 2 3 4 56789	1 2 3 4 56789	1 2 3 4 56789
1 2 3 4 56789	1 2 3 4 56789	1 2 3 4 56789	1 2 3 4 56789	1 2 3 4 56789	1 2 3 4 56789	1 2 3 4 56789	1 2 3 4 56789	1 2 3 4 56789
1 2 3 4 56789	1 2 3 4 56789	1 2 3 4 56789	1 2 3 4 56789	1 2 3 4 56789	1 2 3 4 56789	1 2 3 4 56789	1 2 3 4 56789	1 2 3 4 56789
1 2 3 4 56789	1 2 3 4 56789	1 2 3 4 56789	1 2 3 4 56789	1 2 3 4 56789	1 2 3 4 56789	1 2 3 4 56789	1 2 3 4 56789	1 2 3 4 56789
1 2 3 4 56789	1 2 3 4 56789	1 2 3 4 56789	1 2 3 4 56789	1 2 3 4 56789	1 2 3 4 56789	1 2 3 4 56789	1 2 3 4 56789	1 2 3 4 56789
1 2 3 4 56789	1 2 3 4 56789	1 2 3 4 56789	1 2 3 4 56789	1 2 3 4 56789	1 2 3 4 56789	1 2 3 4 56789	1 2 3 4 56789	1 2 3 4 56789
1 2 3 4 56789	1 2 3 4 56789	1 2 3 4 56789	1 2 3 4 56789	1 2 3 4 56789	1 2 3 4 56789	1 2 3 4 56789	1 2 3 4 56789	1 2 3 4 56789
1 2 3 4 56789	1 2 3 4 56789	1 2 3 4 56789	1 2 3 4 56789	1 2 3 4 56789	1 2 3 4 56789	1 2 3 4 56789	1 2 3 4 56789	1 2 3 4 56789
1 2 3 4 56789	1 2 3 4 56789	1 2 3 4 56789	1 2 3 4 56789	1 2 3 4 56789	1 2 3 4 56789	1 2 3 4 56789	1 2 3 4 56789	1 2 3 4 56789

1 2 3 4 56789	1 2 3 4 56789	1 2 3 4 56789	1 2 3 4 56789	1 2 3 4 56789	1 2 3 4 56789	1 2 3 4 56789	1 2 3 4 56789	1 2 3 4 56789
1 2 3 4 56789	1 2 3 4 56789	1 2 3 4 56789	1 2 3 4 56789	1 2 3 4 56789	1 2 3 4 56789	1 2 3 4 56789	1 2 3 4 56789	1 2 3 4 56789
1 2 3 4 56789	1 2 3 4 56789	1 2 3 4 56789	1 2 3 4 56789	1 2 3 4 56789	1 2 3 4 56789	1 2 3 4 56789	1 2 3 4 56789	1 2 3 4 56789
1 2 3 4 56789	1 2 3 4 56789	1 2 3 4 56789	1 2 3 4 56789	1 2 3 4 56789	1 2 3 4 56789	1 2 3 4 56789	1 2 3 4 56789	1 2 3 4 56789
1 2 3 4 56789	1 2 3 4 56789	1 2 3 4 56789	1 2 3 4 56789	1 2 3 4 56789	1 2 3 4 56789	1 2 3 4 56789	1 2 3 4 56789	1 2 3 4 56789
1 2 3 4 56789	1 2 3 4 56789	1 2 3 4 56789	1 2 3 4 56789	1 2 3 4 56789	1 2 3 4 56789	1 2 3 4 56789	1 2 3 4 56789	1 2 3 4 56789
1 2 3 4 56789	1 2 3 4 56789	1 2 3 4 56789	1 2 3 4 56789	1 2 3 4 56789	1 2 3 4 56789	1 2 3 4 56789	1 2 3 4 56789	1 2 3 4 56789
1 2 3 4 56789	1 2 3 4 56789	1 2 3 4 56789	1 2 3 4 56789	1 2 3 4 56789	1 2 3 4 56789	1 2 3 4 56789	1 2 3 4 56789	1 2 3 4 56789
1 2 3 4 56789	1 2 3 4 56789	1 2 3 4 56789	1 2 3 4 56789	1 2 3 4 56789	1 2 3 4 56789	1 2 3 4 56789	1 2 3 4 56789	1 2 3 4 56789

1 2 3 4 56789	1 2 3 4 56789	1 2 3 4 56789	1 2 3 4 56789	1 2 3 4 56789	1 2 3 4 56789	1 2 3 4 56789	1 2 3 4 56789	1 2 3 4 56789
1 2 3 4 56789	1 2 3 4 56789	1 2 3 4 56789	1 2 3 4 56789	1 2 3 4 56789	1 2 3 4 56789	1 2 3 4 56789	1 2 3 4 56789	1 2 3 4 56789
1 2 3 4 56789	1 2 3 4 56789	1 2 3 4 56789	1 2 3 4 56789	1 2 3 4 56789	1 2 3 4 56789	1 2 3 4 56789	1 2 3 4 56789	1 2 3 4 56789
1 2 3 4 56789	1 2 3 4 56789	1 2 3 4 56789	1 2 3 4 56789	1 2 3 4 56789	1 2 3 4 56789	1 2 3 4 56789	1 2 3 4 56789	1 2 3 4 56789
1 2 3 4 56789	1 2 3 4 56789	1 2 3 4 56789	1 2 3 4 56789	1 2 3 4 56789	1 2 3 4 56789	1 2 3 4 56789	1 2 3 4 56789	1 2 3 4 56789
1 2 3 4 56789	1 2 3 4 56789	1 2 3 4 56789	1 2 3 4 56789	1 2 3 4 56789	1 2 3 4 56789	1 2 3 4 56789	1 2 3 4 56789	1 2 3 4 56789
1 2 3 4 56789	1 2 3 4 56789	1 2 3 4 56789	1 2 3 4 56789	1 2 3 4 56789	1 2 3 4 56789	1 2 3 4 56789	1 2 3 4 56789	1 2 3 4 56789
1 2 3 4 56789	1 2 3 4 56789	1 2 3 4 56789	1 2 3 4 56789	1 2 3 4 56789	1 2 3 4 56789	1 2 3 4 56789	1 2 3 4 56789	1 2 3 4 56789
1 2 3 4 56789	1 2 3 4 56789	1 2 3 4 56789	1 2 3 4 56789	1 2 3 4 56789	1 2 3 4 56789	1 2 3 4 56789	1 2 3 4 56789	1 2 3 4 56789

1 2 3 4 56789	1 2 3 4 56789	1 2 3 4 56789	1 2 3 4 56789	1 2 3 4 56789	1 2 3 4 56789	1 2 3 4 56789	1 2 3 4 56789	1 2 3 4 56789
1 2 3 4 56789	1 2 3 4 56789	1 2 3 4 56789	1 2 3 4 56789	1 2 3 4 56789	1 2 3 4 56789	1 2 3 4 56789	1 2 3 4 56789	1 2 3 4 56789
1 2 3 4 56789	1 2 3 4 56789	1 2 3 4 56789	1 2 3 4 56789	1 2 3 4 56789	1 2 3 4 56789	1 2 3 4 56789	1 2 3 4 56789	1 2 3 4 56789
1 2 3 4 56789	1 2 3 4 56789	1 2 3 4 56789	1 2 3 4 56789	1 2 3 4 56789	1 2 3 4 56789	1 2 3 4 56789	1 2 3 4 56789	1 2 3 4 56789
1 2 3 4 56789	1 2 3 4 56789	1 2 3 4 56789	1 2 3 4 56789	1 2 3 4 56789	1 2 3 4 56789	1 2 3 4 56789	1 2 3 4 56789	1 2 3 4 56789
1 2 3 4 56789	1 2 3 4 56789	1 2 3 4 56789	1 2 3 4 56789	1 2 3 4 56789	1 2 3 4 56789	1 2 3 4 56789	1 2 3 4 56789	1 2 3 4 56789
1 2 3 4 56789	1 2 3 4 56789	1 2 3 4 56789	1 2 3 4 56789	1 2 3 4 56789	1 2 3 4 56789	1 2 3 4 56789	1 2 3 4 56789	1 2 3 4 56789
1 2 3 4 56789	1 2 3 4 56789	1 2 3 4 56789	1 2 3 4 56789	1 2 3 4 56789	1 2 3 4 56789	1 2 3 4 56789	1 2 3 4 56789	1 2 3 4 56789
1 2 3 4 56789	1 2 3 4 56789	1 2 3 4 56789	1 2 3 4 56789	1 2 3 4 56789	1 2 3 4 56789	1 2 3 4 56789	1 2 3 4 56789	1 2 3 4 56789

1234 56789	1234 56789	1234 56789	1234 56789	1234 56789	1234 56789	1234 56789	1234 56789	1234 56789
1234 56789	1234 56789	1234 56789	1234 56789	1234 56789	1234 56789	1234 56789	1234 56789	1234 56789
1234 56789	1234 56789	1234 56789	1234 56789	1234 56789	1234 56789	1234 56789	1234 56789	1234 56789
1234 56789	1234 56789	1234 56789	1234 56789	1234 56789	1234 56789	1234 56789	1234 56789	1234 56789
1234 56789	1234 56789	1234 56789	1234 56789	1234 56789	1234 56789	1234 56789	1234 56789	1234 56789
1234 56789	1234 56789	1234 56789	1234 56789	1234 56789	1234 56789	1234 56789	1234 56789	1234 56789
1234 56789	1234 56789	1234 56789	1234 56789	1234 56789	1234 56789	1234 56789	1234 56789	1234 56789
1234 56789	1234 56789	1234 56789	1234 56789	1234 56789	1234 56789	1234 56789	1234 56789	1234 56789
1234 56789	1234 56789	1234 56789	1234 56789	1234 56789	1234 56789	1234 56789	1234 56789	1234 56789

1 2 3 4 56789	1 2 3 4 56789	1 2 3 4 56789	1 2 3 4 56789	1 2 3 4 56789	1 2 3 4 56789	1 2 3 4 56789	1 2 3 4 56789	1 2 3 4 56789
1 2 3 4 56789	1 2 3 4 56789	1 2 3 4 56789	1 2 3 4 56789	1 2 3 4 56789	1 2 3 4 56789	1 2 3 4 56789	1 2 3 4 56789	1 2 3 4 56789
1 2 3 4 56789	1 2 3 4 56789	1 2 3 4 56789	1 2 3 4 56789	1 2 3 4 56789	1 2 3 4 56789	1 2 3 4 56789	1 2 3 4 56789	1 2 3 4 56789
1 2 3 4 56789	1 2 3 4 56789	1 2 3 4 56789	1 2 3 4 56789	1 2 3 4 56789	1 2 3 4 56789	1 2 3 4 56789	1 2 3 4 56789	1 2 3 4 56789
1 2 3 4 56789	1 2 3 4 56789	1 2 3 4 56789	1 2 3 4 56789	1 2 3 4 56789	1 2 3 4 56789	1 2 3 4 56789	1 2 3 4 56789	1 2 3 4 56789
1 2 3 4 56789	1 2 3 4 56789	1 2 3 4 56789	1 2 3 4 56789	1 2 3 4 56789	1 2 3 4 56789	1 2 3 4 56789	1 2 3 4 56789	1 2 3 4 56789
1 2 3 4 56789	1 2 3 4 56789	1 2 3 4 56789	1 2 3 4 56789	1 2 3 4 56789	1 2 3 4 56789	1 2 3 4 56789	1 2 3 4 56789	1 2 3 4 56789
1 2 3 4 56789	1 2 3 4 56789	1 2 3 4 56789	1 2 3 4 56789	1 2 3 4 56789	1 2 3 4 56789	1 2 3 4 56789	1 2 3 4 56789	1 2 3 4 56789
1 2 3 4 56789	1 2 3 4 56789	1 2 3 4 56789	1 2 3 4 56789	1 2 3 4 56789	1 2 3 4 56789	1 2 3 4 56789	1 2 3 4 56789	1 2 3 4 56789

1 2 3 4 56789	1 2 3 4 56789	1 2 3 4 56789	1 2 3 4 56789	1 2 3 4 56789	1 2 3 4 56789	1 2 3 4 56789	1 2 3 4 56789	1 2 3 4 56789
1 2 3 4 56789	1 2 3 4 56789	1 2 3 4 56789	1 2 3 4 56789	1 2 3 4 56789	1 2 3 4 56789	1 2 3 4 56789	1 2 3 4 56789	1 2 3 4 56789
1 2 3 4 56789	1 2 3 4 56789	1 2 3 4 56789	1 2 3 4 56789	1 2 3 4 56789	1 2 3 4 56789	1 2 3 4 56789	1 2 3 4 56789	1 2 3 4 56789
1 2 3 4 56789	1 2 3 4 56789	1 2 3 4 56789	1 2 3 4 56789	1 2 3 4 56789	1 2 3 4 56789	1 2 3 4 56789	1 2 3 4 56789	1 2 3 4 56789
1 2 3 4 56789	1 2 3 4 56789	1 2 3 4 56789	1 2 3 4 56789	1 2 3 4 56789	1 2 3 4 56789	1 2 3 4 56789	1 2 3 4 56789	1 2 3 4 56789
1 2 3 4 56789	1 2 3 4 56789	1 2 3 4 56789	1 2 3 4 56789	1 2 3 4 56789	1 2 3 4 56789	1 2 3 4 56789	1 2 3 4 56789	1 2 3 4 56789
1 2 3 4 56789	1 2 3 4 56789	1 2 3 4 56789	1 2 3 4 56789	1 2 3 4 56789	1 2 3 4 56789	1 2 3 4 56789	1 2 3 4 56789	1 2 3 4 56789
1 2 3 4 56789	1 2 3 4 56789	1 2 3 4 56789	1 2 3 4 56789	1 2 3 4 56789	1 2 3 4 56789	1 2 3 4 56789	1 2 3 4 56789	1 2 3 4 56789
1 2 3 4 56789	1 2 3 4 56789	1 2 3 4 56789	1 2 3 4 56789	1 2 3 4 56789	1 2 3 4 56789	1 2 3 4 56789	1 2 3 4 56789	1 2 3 4 56789

1 2 3 4 56789	1 2 3 4 56789	1 2 3 4 56789	1 2 3 4 56789	1 2 3 4 56789	1 2 3 4 56789	1 2 3 4 56789	1 2 3 4 56789	1 2 3 4 56789
1 2 3 4 56789	1 2 3 4 56789	1 2 3 4 56789	1 2 3 4 56789	1 2 3 4 56789	1 2 3 4 56789	1 2 3 4 56789	1 2 3 4 56789	1 2 3 4 56789
1 2 3 4 56789	1 2 3 4 56789	1 2 3 4 56789	1 2 3 4 56789	1 2 3 4 56789	1 2 3 4 56789	1 2 3 4 56789	1 2 3 4 56789	1 2 3 4 56789
1 2 3 4 56789	1 2 3 4 56789	1 2 3 4 56789	1 2 3 4 56789	1 2 3 4 56789	1 2 3 4 56789	1 2 3 4 56789	1 2 3 4 56789	1 2 3 4 56789
1 2 3 4 56789	1 2 3 4 56789	1 2 3 4 56789	1 2 3 4 56789	1 2 3 4 56789	1 2 3 4 56789	1 2 3 4 56789	1 2 3 4 56789	1 2 3 4 56789
1 2 3 4 56789	1 2 3 4 56789	1 2 3 4 56789	1 2 3 4 56789	1 2 3 4 56789	1 2 3 4 56789	1 2 3 4 56789	1 2 3 4 56789	1 2 3 4 56789
1 2 3 4 56789	1 2 3 4 56789	1 2 3 4 56789	1 2 3 4 56789	1 2 3 4 56789	1 2 3 4 56789	1 2 3 4 56789	1 2 3 4 56789	1 2 3 4 56789
1 2 3 4 56789	1 2 3 4 56789	1 2 3 4 56789	1 2 3 4 56789	1 2 3 4 56789	1 2 3 4 56789	1 2 3 4 56789	1 2 3 4 56789	1 2 3 4 56789
1 2 3 4 56789	1 2 3 4 56789	1 2 3 4 56789	1 2 3 4 56789	1 2 3 4 56789	1 2 3 4 56789	1 2 3 4 56789	1 2 3 4 56789	1 2 3 4 56789

1 2 3 4 56789	1 2 3 4 56789	1 2 3 4 56789	1 2 3 4 56789	1 2 3 4 56789	1 2 3 4 56789	1 2 3 4 56789	1 2 3 4 56789	1 2 3 4 56789
1 2 3 4 56789	1 2 3 4 56789	1 2 3 4 56789	1 2 3 4 56789	1 2 3 4 56789	1 2 3 4 56789	1 2 3 4 56789	1 2 3 4 56789	1 2 3 4 56789
1 2 3 4 56789	1 2 3 4 56789	1 2 3 4 56789	1 2 3 4 56789	1 2 3 4 56789	1 2 3 4 56789	1 2 3 4 56789	1 2 3 4 56789	1 2 3 4 56789
1 2 3 4 56789	1 2 3 4 56789	1 2 3 4 56789	1 2 3 4 56789	1 2 3 4 56789	1 2 3 4 56789	1 2 3 4 56789	1 2 3 4 56789	1 2 3 4 56789
1 2 3 4 56789	1 2 3 4 56789	1 2 3 4 56789	1 2 3 4 56789	1 2 3 4 56789	1 2 3 4 56789	1 2 3 4 56789	1 2 3 4 56789	1 2 3 4 56789
1 2 3 4 56789	1 2 3 4 56789	1 2 3 4 56789	1 2 3 4 56789	1 2 3 4 56789	1 2 3 4 56789	1 2 3 4 56789	1 2 3 4 56789	1 2 3 4 56789
1 2 3 4 56789	1 2 3 4 56789	1 2 3 4 56789	1 2 3 4 56789	1 2 3 4 56789	1 2 3 4 56789	1 2 3 4 56789	1 2 3 4 56789	1 2 3 4 56789
1 2 3 4 56789	1 2 3 4 56789	1 2 3 4 56789	1 2 3 4 56789	1 2 3 4 56789	1 2 3 4 56789	1 2 3 4 56789	1 2 3 4 56789	1 2 3 4 56789
1 2 3 4 56789	1 2 3 4 56789	1 2 3 4 56789	1 2 3 4 56789	1 2 3 4 56789	1 2 3 4 56789	1 2 3 4 56789	1 2 3 4 56789	1 2 3 4 56789

1 2 3 4 56789	1 2 3 4 56789	1 2 3 4 56789	1 2 3 4 56789	1 2 3 4 56789	1 2 3 4 56789	1 2 3 4 56789	1 2 3 4 56789	1 2 3 4 56789
1 2 3 4 56789	1 2 3 4 56789	1 2 3 4 56789	1 2 3 4 56789	1 2 3 4 56789	1 2 3 4 56789	1 2 3 4 56789	1 2 3 4 56789	1 2 3 4 56789
1 2 3 4 56789	1 2 3 4 56789	1 2 3 4 56789	1 2 3 4 56789	1 2 3 4 56789	1 2 3 4 56789	1 2 3 4 56789	1 2 3 4 56789	1 2 3 4 56789
1 2 3 4 56789	1 2 3 4 56789	1 2 3 4 56789	1 2 3 4 56789	1 2 3 4 56789	1 2 3 4 56789	1 2 3 4 56789	1 2 3 4 56789	1 2 3 4 56789
1 2 3 4 56789	1 2 3 4 56789	1 2 3 4 56789	1 2 3 4 56789	1 2 3 4 56789	1 2 3 4 56789	1 2 3 4 56789	1 2 3 4 56789	1 2 3 4 56789
1 2 3 4 56789	1 2 3 4 56789	1 2 3 4 56789	1 2 3 4 56789	1 2 3 4 56789	1 2 3 4 56789	1 2 3 4 56789	1 2 3 4 56789	1 2 3 4 56789
1 2 3 4 56789	1 2 3 4 56789	1 2 3 4 56789	1 2 3 4 56789	1 2 3 4 56789	1 2 3 4 56789	1 2 3 4 56789	1 2 3 4 56789	1 2 3 4 56789
1 2 3 4 56789	1 2 3 4 56789	1 2 3 4 56789	1 2 3 4 56789	1 2 3 4 56789	1 2 3 4 56789	1 2 3 4 56789	1 2 3 4 56789	1 2 3 4 56789
1 2 3 4 56789	1 2 3 4 56789	1 2 3 4 56789	1 2 3 4 56789	1 2 3 4 56789	1 2 3 4 56789	1 2 3 4 56789	1 2 3 4 56789	1 2 3 4 56789

1 2 3 4 56789	1 2 3 4 56789	1 2 3 4 56789	1 2 3 4 56789	1 2 3 4 56789	1 2 3 4 56789	1 2 3 4 56789	1 2 3 4 56789	1 2 3 4 56789
1 2 3 4 56789	1 2 3 4 56789	1 2 3 4 56789	1 2 3 4 56789	1 2 3 4 56789	1 2 3 4 56789	1 2 3 4 56789	1 2 3 4 56789	1 2 3 4 56789
1 2 3 4 56789	1 2 3 4 56789	1 2 3 4 56789	1 2 3 4 56789	1 2 3 4 56789	1 2 3 4 56789	1 2 3 4 56789	1 2 3 4 56789	1 2 3 4 56789
1 2 3 4 56789	1 2 3 4 56789	1 2 3 4 56789	1 2 3 4 56789	1 2 3 4 56789	1 2 3 4 56789	1 2 3 4 56789	1 2 3 4 56789	1 2 3 4 56789
1 2 3 4 56789	1 2 3 4 56789	1 2 3 4 56789	1 2 3 4 56789	1 2 3 4 56789	1 2 3 4 56789	1 2 3 4 56789	1 2 3 4 56789	1 2 3 4 56789
1 2 3 4 56789	1 2 3 4 56789	1 2 3 4 56789	1 2 3 4 56789	1 2 3 4 56789	1 2 3 4 56789	1 2 3 4 56789	1 2 3 4 56789	1 2 3 4 56789
1 2 3 4 56789	1 2 3 4 56789	1 2 3 4 56789	1 2 3 4 56789	1 2 3 4 56789	1 2 3 4 56789	1 2 3 4 56789	1 2 3 4 56789	1 2 3 4 56789
1 2 3 4 56789	1 2 3 4 56789	1 2 3 4 56789	1 2 3 4 56789	1 2 3 4 56789	1 2 3 4 56789	1 2 3 4 56789	1 2 3 4 56789	1 2 3 4 56789
1 2 3 4 56789	1 2 3 4 56789	1 2 3 4 56789	1 2 3 4 56789	1 2 3 4 56789	1 2 3 4 56789	1 2 3 4 56789	1 2 3 4 56789	1 2 3 4 56789

1 2 3 4 56789	1 2 3 4 56789	1 2 3 4 56789	1 2 3 4 56789	1 2 3 4 56789	1 2 3 4 56789	1 2 3 4 56789	1 2 3 4 56789	1 2 3 4 56789
1 2 3 4 56789	1 2 3 4 56789	1 2 3 4 56789	1 2 3 4 56789	1 2 3 4 56789	1 2 3 4 56789	1 2 3 4 56789	1 2 3 4 56789	1 2 3 4 56789
1 2 3 4 56789	1 2 3 4 56789	1 2 3 4 56789	1 2 3 4 56789	1 2 3 4 56789	1 2 3 4 56789	1 2 3 4 56789	1 2 3 4 56789	1 2 3 4 56789
1 2 3 4 56789	1 2 3 4 56789	1 2 3 4 56789	1 2 3 4 56789	1 2 3 4 56789	1 2 3 4 56789	1 2 3 4 56789	1 2 3 4 56789	1 2 3 4 56789
1 2 3 4 56789	1 2 3 4 56789	1 2 3 4 56789	1 2 3 4 56789	1 2 3 4 56789	1 2 3 4 56789	1 2 3 4 56789	1 2 3 4 56789	1 2 3 4 56789
1 2 3 4 56789	1 2 3 4 56789	1 2 3 4 56789	1 2 3 4 56789	1 2 3 4 56789	1 2 3 4 56789	1 2 3 4 56789	1 2 3 4 56789	1 2 3 4 56789
1 2 3 4 56789	1 2 3 4 56789	1 2 3 4 56789	1 2 3 4 56789	1 2 3 4 56789	1 2 3 4 56789	1 2 3 4 56789	1 2 3 4 56789	1 2 3 4 56789
1 2 3 4 56789	1 2 3 4 56789	1 2 3 4 56789	1 2 3 4 56789	1 2 3 4 56789	1 2 3 4 56789	1 2 3 4 56789	1 2 3 4 56789	1 2 3 4 56789
1 2 3 4 56789	1 2 3 4 56789	1 2 3 4 56789	1 2 3 4 56789	1 2 3 4 56789	1 2 3 4 56789	1 2 3 4 56789	1 2 3 4 56789	1 2 3 4 56789

1 2 3 4 56789	1 2 3 4 56789	1 2 3 4 56789	1 2 3 4 56789	1 2 3 4 56789	1 2 3 4 56789	1 2 3 4 56789	1 2 3 4 56789	1 2 3 4 56789
1 2 3 4 56789	1 2 3 4 56789	1 2 3 4 56789	1 2 3 4 56789	1 2 3 4 56789	1 2 3 4 56789	1 2 3 4 56789	1 2 3 4 56789	1 2 3 4 56789
1 2 3 4 56789	1 2 3 4 56789	1 2 3 4 56789	1 2 3 4 56789	1 2 3 4 56789	1 2 3 4 56789	1 2 3 4 56789	1 2 3 4 56789	1 2 3 4 56789
1 2 3 4 56789	1 2 3 4 56789	1 2 3 4 56789	1 2 3 4 56789	1 2 3 4 56789	1 2 3 4 56789	1 2 3 4 56789	1 2 3 4 56789	1 2 3 4 56789
1 2 3 4 56789	1 2 3 4 56789	1 2 3 4 56789	1 2 3 4 56789	1 2 3 4 56789	1 2 3 4 56789	1 2 3 4 56789	1 2 3 4 56789	1 2 3 4 56789
1 2 3 4 56789	1 2 3 4 56789	1 2 3 4 56789	1 2 3 4 56789	1 2 3 4 56789	1 2 3 4 56789	1 2 3 4 56789	1 2 3 4 56789	1 2 3 4 56789
1 2 3 4 56789	1 2 3 4 56789	1 2 3 4 56789	1 2 3 4 56789	1 2 3 4 56789	1 2 3 4 56789	1 2 3 4 56789	1 2 3 4 56789	1 2 3 4 56789
1 2 3 4 56789	1 2 3 4 56789	1 2 3 4 56789	1 2 3 4 56789	1 2 3 4 56789	1 2 3 4 56789	1 2 3 4 56789	1 2 3 4 56789	1 2 3 4 56789
1 2 3 4 56789	1 2 3 4 56789	1 2 3 4 56789	1 2 3 4 56789	1 2 3 4 56789	1 2 3 4 56789	1 2 3 4 56789	1 2 3 4 56789	1 2 3 4 56789

1 2 3 4 56789	1 2 3 4 56789	1 2 3 4 56789	1 2 3 4 56789	1 2 3 4 56789	1 2 3 4 56789	1 2 3 4 56789	1 2 3 4 56789	1 2 3 4 56789
1 2 3 4 56789	1 2 3 4 56789	1 2 3 4 56789	1 2 3 4 56789	1 2 3 4 56789	1 2 3 4 56789	1 2 3 4 56789	1 2 3 4 56789	1 2 3 4 56789
1 2 3 4 56789	1 2 3 4 56789	1 2 3 4 56789	1 2 3 4 56789	1 2 3 4 56789	1 2 3 4 56789	1 2 3 4 56789	1 2 3 4 56789	1 2 3 4 56789
1 2 3 4 56789	1 2 3 4 56789	1 2 3 4 56789	1 2 3 4 56789	1 2 3 4 56789	1 2 3 4 56789	1 2 3 4 56789	1 2 3 4 56789	1 2 3 4 56789
1 2 3 4 56789	1 2 3 4 56789	1 2 3 4 56789	1 2 3 4 56789	1 2 3 4 56789	1 2 3 4 56789	1 2 3 4 56789	1 2 3 4 56789	1 2 3 4 56789
1 2 3 4 56789	1 2 3 4 56789	1 2 3 4 56789	1 2 3 4 56789	1 2 3 4 56789	1 2 3 4 56789	1 2 3 4 56789	1 2 3 4 56789	1 2 3 4 56789
1 2 3 4 56789	1 2 3 4 56789	1 2 3 4 56789	1 2 3 4 56789	1 2 3 4 56789	1 2 3 4 56789	1 2 3 4 56789	1 2 3 4 56789	1 2 3 4 56789
1 2 3 4 56789	1 2 3 4 56789	1 2 3 4 56789	1 2 3 4 56789	1 2 3 4 56789	1 2 3 4 56789	1 2 3 4 56789	1 2 3 4 56789	1 2 3 4 56789
1 2 3 4 56789	1 2 3 4 56789	1 2 3 4 56789	1 2 3 4 56789	1 2 3 4 56789	1 2 3 4 56789	1 2 3 4 56789	1 2 3 4 56789	1 2 3 4 56789

1 2 3 4 56789	1 2 3 4 56789	1 2 3 4 56789	1 2 3 4 56789	1 2 3 4 56789	1 2 3 4 56789	1 2 3 4 56789	1 2 3 4 56789	1 2 3 4 56789
1 2 3 4 56789	1 2 3 4 56789	1 2 3 4 56789	1 2 3 4 56789	1 2 3 4 56789	1 2 3 4 56789	1 2 3 4 56789	1 2 3 4 56789	1 2 3 4 56789
1 2 3 4 56789	1 2 3 4 56789	1 2 3 4 56789	1 2 3 4 56789	1 2 3 4 56789	1 2 3 4 56789	1 2 3 4 56789	1 2 3 4 56789	1 2 3 4 56789
1 2 3 4 56789	1 2 3 4 56789	1 2 3 4 56789	1 2 3 4 56789	1 2 3 4 56789	1 2 3 4 56789	1 2 3 4 56789	1 2 3 4 56789	1 2 3 4 56789
1 2 3 4 56789	1 2 3 4 56789	1 2 3 4 56789	1 2 3 4 56789	1 2 3 4 56789	1 2 3 4 56789	1 2 3 4 56789	1 2 3 4 56789	1 2 3 4 56789
1 2 3 4 56789	1 2 3 4 56789	1 2 3 4 56789	1 2 3 4 56789	1 2 3 4 56789	1 2 3 4 56789	1 2 3 4 56789	1 2 3 4 56789	1 2 3 4 56789
1 2 3 4 56789	1 2 3 4 56789	1 2 3 4 56789	1 2 3 4 56789	1 2 3 4 56789	1 2 3 4 56789	1 2 3 4 56789	1 2 3 4 56789	1 2 3 4 56789
1 2 3 4 56789	1 2 3 4 56789	1 2 3 4 56789	1 2 3 4 56789	1 2 3 4 56789	1 2 3 4 56789	1 2 3 4 56789	1 2 3 4 56789	1 2 3 4 56789
1 2 3 4 56789	1 2 3 4 56789	1 2 3 4 56789	1 2 3 4 56789	1 2 3 4 56789	1 2 3 4 56789	1 2 3 4 56789	1 2 3 4 56789	1 2 3 4 56789

1 2 3 4 56789	1 2 3 4 56789	1 2 3 4 56789	1 2 3 4 56789	1 2 3 4 56789	1 2 3 4 56789	1 2 3 4 56789	1 2 3 4 56789	1 2 3 4 56789
1 2 3 4 56789	1 2 3 4 56789	1 2 3 4 56789	1 2 3 4 56789	1 2 3 4 56789	1 2 3 4 56789	1 2 3 4 56789	1 2 3 4 56789	1 2 3 4 56789
1 2 3 4 56789	1 2 3 4 56789	1 2 3 4 56789	1 2 3 4 56789	1 2 3 4 56789	1 2 3 4 56789	1 2 3 4 56789	1 2 3 4 56789	1 2 3 4 56789
1 2 3 4 56789	1 2 3 4 56789	1 2 3 4 56789	1 2 3 4 56789	1 2 3 4 56789	1 2 3 4 56789	1 2 3 4 56789	1 2 3 4 56789	1 2 3 4 56789
1 2 3 4 56789	1 2 3 4 56789	1 2 3 4 56789	1 2 3 4 56789	1 2 3 4 56789	1 2 3 4 56789	1 2 3 4 56789	1 2 3 4 56789	1 2 3 4 56789
1 2 3 4 56789	1 2 3 4 56789	1 2 3 4 56789	1 2 3 4 56789	1 2 3 4 56789	1 2 3 4 56789	1 2 3 4 56789	1 2 3 4 56789	1 2 3 4 56789
1 2 3 4 56789	1 2 3 4 56789	1 2 3 4 56789	1 2 3 4 56789	1 2 3 4 56789	1 2 3 4 56789	1 2 3 4 56789	1 2 3 4 56789	1 2 3 4 56789
1 2 3 4 56789	1 2 3 4 56789	1 2 3 4 56789	1 2 3 4 56789	1 2 3 4 56789	1 2 3 4 56789	1 2 3 4 56789	1 2 3 4 56789	1 2 3 4 56789
1 2 3 4 56789	1 2 3 4 56789	1 2 3 4 56789	1 2 3 4 56789	1 2 3 4 56789	1 2 3 4 56789	1 2 3 4 56789	1 2 3 4 56789	1 2 3 4 56789

1 2 3 4 56789	1 2 3 4 56789	1 2 3 4 56789	1 2 3 4 56789	1 2 3 4 56789	1 2 3 4 56789	1 2 3 4 56789	1 2 3 4 56789	1 2 3 4 56789
1 2 3 4 56789	1 2 3 4 56789	1 2 3 4 56789	1 2 3 4 56789	1 2 3 4 56789	1 2 3 4 56789	1 2 3 4 56789	1 2 3 4 56789	1 2 3 4 56789
1 2 3 4 56789	1 2 3 4 56789	1 2 3 4 56789	1 2 3 4 56789	1 2 3 4 56789	1 2 3 4 56789	1 2 3 4 56789	1 2 3 4 56789	1 2 3 4 56789
1 2 3 4 56789	1 2 3 4 56789	1 2 3 4 56789	1 2 3 4 56789	1 2 3 4 56789	1 2 3 4 56789	1 2 3 4 56789	1 2 3 4 56789	1 2 3 4 56789
1 2 3 4 56789	1 2 3 4 56789	1 2 3 4 56789	1 2 3 4 56789	1 2 3 4 56789	1 2 3 4 56789	1 2 3 4 56789	1 2 3 4 56789	1 2 3 4 56789
1 2 3 4 56789	1 2 3 4 56789	1 2 3 4 56789	1 2 3 4 56789	1 2 3 4 56789	1 2 3 4 56789	1 2 3 4 56789	1 2 3 4 56789	1 2 3 4 56789
1 2 3 4 56789	1 2 3 4 56789	1 2 3 4 56789	1 2 3 4 56789	1 2 3 4 56789	1 2 3 4 56789	1 2 3 4 56789	1 2 3 4 56789	1 2 3 4 56789
1 2 3 4 56789	1 2 3 4 56789	1 2 3 4 56789	1 2 3 4 56789	1 2 3 4 56789	1 2 3 4 56789	1 2 3 4 56789	1 2 3 4 56789	1 2 3 4 56789
1 2 3 4 56789	1 2 3 4 56789	1 2 3 4 56789	1 2 3 4 56789	1 2 3 4 56789	1 2 3 4 56789	1 2 3 4 56789	1 2 3 4 56789	1 2 3 4 56789

1 2 3 4 56789	1 2 3 4 56789	1 2 3 4 56789	1 2 3 4 56789	1 2 3 4 56789	1 2 3 4 56789	1 2 3 4 56789	1 2 3 4 56789	1 2 3 4 56789
1 2 3 4 56789	1 2 3 4 56789	1 2 3 4 56789	1 2 3 4 56789	1 2 3 4 56789	1 2 3 4 56789	1 2 3 4 56789	1 2 3 4 56789	1 2 3 4 56789
1 2 3 4 56789	1 2 3 4 56789	1 2 3 4 56789	1 2 3 4 56789	1 2 3 4 56789	1 2 3 4 56789	1 2 3 4 56789	1 2 3 4 56789	1 2 3 4 56789
1 2 3 4 56789	1 2 3 4 56789	1 2 3 4 56789	1 2 3 4 56789	1 2 3 4 56789	1 2 3 4 56789	1 2 3 4 56789	1 2 3 4 56789	1 2 3 4 56789
1 2 3 4 56789	1 2 3 4 56789	1 2 3 4 56789	1 2 3 4 56789	1 2 3 4 56789	1 2 3 4 56789	1 2 3 4 56789	1 2 3 4 56789	1 2 3 4 56789
1 2 3 4 56789	1 2 3 4 56789	1 2 3 4 56789	1 2 3 4 56789	1 2 3 4 56789	1 2 3 4 56789	1 2 3 4 56789	1 2 3 4 56789	1 2 3 4 56789
1 2 3 4 56789	1 2 3 4 56789	1 2 3 4 56789	1 2 3 4 56789	1 2 3 4 56789	1 2 3 4 56789	1 2 3 4 56789	1 2 3 4 56789	1 2 3 4 56789
1 2 3 4 56789	1 2 3 4 56789	1 2 3 4 56789	1 2 3 4 56789	1 2 3 4 56789	1 2 3 4 56789	1 2 3 4 56789	1 2 3 4 56789	1 2 3 4 56789
1 2 3 4 56789	1 2 3 4 56789	1 2 3 4 56789	1 2 3 4 56789	1 2 3 4 56789	1 2 3 4 56789	1 2 3 4 56789	1 2 3 4 56789	1 2 3 4 56789

1 2 3 4 56789	1 2 3 4 56789	1 2 3 4 56789	1 2 3 4 56789	1 2 3 4 56789	1 2 3 4 56789	1 2 3 4 56789	1 2 3 4 56789	1 2 3 4 56789
1 2 3 4 56789	1 2 3 4 56789	1 2 3 4 56789	1 2 3 4 56789	1 2 3 4 56789	1 2 3 4 56789	1 2 3 4 56789	1 2 3 4 56789	1 2 3 4 56789
1 2 3 4 56789	1 2 3 4 56789	1 2 3 4 56789	1 2 3 4 56789	1 2 3 4 56789	1 2 3 4 56789	1 2 3 4 56789	1 2 3 4 56789	1 2 3 4 56789
1 2 3 4 56789	1 2 3 4 56789	1 2 3 4 56789	1 2 3 4 56789	1 2 3 4 56789	1 2 3 4 56789	1 2 3 4 56789	1 2 3 4 56789	1 2 3 4 56789
1 2 3 4 56789	1 2 3 4 56789	1 2 3 4 56789	1 2 3 4 56789	1 2 3 4 56789	1 2 3 4 56789	1 2 3 4 56789	1 2 3 4 56789	1 2 3 4 56789
1 2 3 4 56789	1 2 3 4 56789	1 2 3 4 56789	1 2 3 4 56789	1 2 3 4 56789	1 2 3 4 56789	1 2 3 4 56789	1 2 3 4 56789	1 2 3 4 56789
1 2 3 4 56789	1 2 3 4 56789	1 2 3 4 56789	1 2 3 4 56789	1 2 3 4 56789	1 2 3 4 56789	1 2 3 4 56789	1 2 3 4 56789	1 2 3 4 56789
1 2 3 4 56789	1 2 3 4 56789	1 2 3 4 56789	1 2 3 4 56789	1 2 3 4 56789	1 2 3 4 56789	1 2 3 4 56789	1 2 3 4 56789	1 2 3 4 56789
1 2 3 4 56789	1 2 3 4 56789	1 2 3 4 56789	1 2 3 4 56789	1 2 3 4 56789	1 2 3 4 56789	1 2 3 4 56789	1 2 3 4 56789	1 2 3 4 56789